Measurement-Based Evaluation of Teacher Performance

Measurement-Based Evaluation
of
Teacher Performance

An Empirical Approach

Donald M. Medley
University of Virginia

Homer Coker
Georgia State University

Robert S. Soar
University of Florida

Longman

New York & London

Measurement-Based Teacher Evaluation
An Empirical Approach

Longman Inc., 1560 Broadway, New York, N.Y. 10036
Associated companies, branches, and representatives
throughout the world.

Developmental Editor: Lane Akers
Editorial and Design Supervisor: Thomas Bacher
Production Supervisor: Ferne Y. Kawahara

Library of Congress Cataloging in Publication Data

Medley, Donald M. (Donald Mathias).
    Measurement based evaluation of teacher performance.
    Bibliography: p.
    Includes index.
    1. Teachers—United States—Rating of.   I. Coker,
Homer   II. Soar, Robert S.
III. Title.
LB2838.C59 1984   371.1′44′0973   83-17570
ISBN 0-582-28502-X

Manufactured in the United States of America
Printing: 9 8 7 6 5 4 3 2 1   Year: 92 91 90 89 88 87 86 85 84

This book is respectfully dedicated to the teachers of America who are surely among the more extensively and intensively

supervised

evaluated

researched

underpaid

and *overworked*

body of professionals in the world. In spite of it all, they continue to educate the youth of America.

Contents

PART I

THE STATE OF THE ART OF TEACHER EVALUATION

PART II

PROCEDURES FOR MEASURING TEACHER PERFORMANCE

CHAPTER 5

Structured Observation Systems   77

CHAPTER 6

Defining the Task to Be Performed   111

CHAPTER 7

Obtaining the Record   125

CHAPTER 8

Scoring the Record   143

PART III

EVALUATION: THE FINAL STEP

Figures

Foreword

B. Othanel Smith

Before the present century, it was widely held that the student was responsible for learning; that the responsibility of the teacher was to hear recitations and to maintain order. Today, almost the opposite view is held; that the teacher is at fault if the student does not learn. While pedagogical literature abounds with opinions and research evidence that the effects of competent instruction are often neutralized by the poverty of the experience and low aspirations of students, still it is generally believed that lack of learning is attributable to flawed instruction.

Placing the responsibility for learning squarely on the teacher's shoulders was accompanied by schemes to evaluate teachers. Very early in this century, rating scales, crude to be sure, were devised for evaluating an individual's ability to teach. Rating scales are now abundant and the supply is likely to increase as state after state mandates the evaluation of both experienced and beginning teachers. Yet there is no comprehensive systematic treatment of the problems of constructing instruments to measure teacher performance. This book fills that void.

The authors present a broad and scholarly treatment of the measurement of classroom performance. They analyze the problems, pitfalls, procedures, and techniques of instrument development. They draw a clear distinction between rating scales and systematic observation measurement, and warn us of the consequences of using rating scales as though they were dependable measures of teacher performance. They define basic terms commonly misused: competency, competence, performance, and effectiveness. They make a compelling case against student achievement as a criterion of teacher evaluation. They deal critically and constructively with the sources of items for an observation schedule: consensus among knowledgeable persons, existing instruments, and findings of research on effective teaching. They deal with ethnographic and ecological modes of observing teacher behavior. They treat the technical problems of establishing the validity, reliability, and generalizability of observation instruments. Not since the classic paper by Medley and Mitzel on systematic observation in the first edition of the *Handbook of Research on Teaching* has reliability been so thoroughly analysed, not to mention other basic measurement concepts.

It is almost axiomatic that a state or school district that requires performance evaluation for admission to the profession, or for tenure and promotion, is thereby obligated to see that its instruments of measurement meet the highest standards of exactitude. This obligation, and the strong trend toward mandated evaluation, augments the significance of this timely book by the leading authorities on systematic observation of classroom performance. These authors have been in the thick of instrument development and they write out of a depth of experience and information that enables them to express basic concepts and principles clearly and succinctly. In view of its comprehensive and analytic character, it seems certain that this book will prove a scholarly and valuable addition to the literature on teacher evaluation.

Acknowledgments

In any project such as this, the help, support, and encouragement of others is always an important element, and this book is no exception. Two of our wives have been major contributors; both Ruth and Joan have participated actively in the process of writing and editing. From beginning to end, Bunnie Smith has been invaluable, offering sage advice, encouragement, and even gentle reproaching to get on with it. Judy Skipper has typed and retyped successive drafts, rapidly and accurately, with good cheer and even enthusiasm at times. Others, so numerous that if we name them we will surely leave someone out, have read and reacted to portions of the draft with insightful comments and reactions to "turgid prose." You know who you are. We appreciate your help and are grateful to you.

Donald M. Medley
Homer Coker
Robert S. Soar

Measurement-Based Evaluation
of
Teacher Performance

Part I

The State of the Art of Teacher Evaluation

1

Introduction

When you think of the best teacher and the worst teacher you ever had, how do you make the choice? Is it on the basis of how you felt about that particular teacher when you were in class? If being there felt good, does that mean the teacher was a good one; and if not, was she* a poor one? Is the judgment based on how much the teacher seemed to know about the subject matter? Or, is it based on how broadly informed the teacher was? Did you share in making decisions about what happened in the classroom? If you did, is that good or bad? Was there a great deal of physical activity and movement in that classroom? Is that good or bad? Or was the classroom closely organized and task oriented? Was the teacher a likeable person? Was she always on time? Well organized? Well groomed? Was she courteous to students? Is that important? Do your more important impressions depend on how old you were at the time or what the teacher was trying to teach you? Or does your choice of the best teacher depend on how much her pupils seemed to learn from her—on their gains on tests of achievement?

Now think of the best and the worst physician you have ever consulted. How do you make this choice? Does it depend on how

---

* To avoid pronoun tangles and to increase the clarity of our discussion, throughout this volume we shall use feminine pronouns to refer to teachers and masculine ones to refer to pupils, observers, and other secondary figures. No slight upon members of either sex is intended nor should any be inferred.

3

comfortable you felt with that physician—on how sympathetic and interested in your feelings he was? On how clean and smooth running his office was, or how punctual and neat he was? Or does it depend on how much confidence he inspired, how much he seemed to know about the practice of medicine, how modern his equipment was (and how much of it he used)? Or does it depend on how many of his patients he treated successfully—on how many of those who had serious illnesses he cured?

Finally, think of the best and the worst plumber you have ever known. How do you make this choice? Does it depend on how courteous he was—on how much sympathy and interest he showed in your problem? On how neat he and his truck were? Or does it depend on how much self-confidence he showed, on how much he seemed to know about plumbing, on the tools and equipment he had and how skillfully he used them? Or does it depend on how well the plumbing worked after he was gone—and for how long?

Reflecting on these choices should emphasize two important points often forgotten. One is that most people know too little about either medicine or plumbing to be able to evaluate either practitioner on the basis of how well he knows his business or whether he is using the best procedures available. This is a point with which most people will agree in relation to most occupations; most people agree that they know too little about medicine, dentistry, law, plumbing, automobile engines, or electronics to evaluate practitioners in these areas on the basis of the procedures they follow.

But this point is not widely accepted as it relates to the practice of teaching. Almost any lay person will make the choice we asked for between the best and worst teacher without hesitation, and will base it, not on the results the teacher gets, but on how she behaves in her classroom. Everyone seems to know the best way to teach.

This curious delusion has a good deal to do with the chaotic state of teacher evaluation today, mainly because it is strongly shared by teacher educators, school administrators, and others responsible for formal evaluation of teachers. The whole art of teacher evaluation up to the present consists of obtaining someone's subjective judgment of how "good" a teacher is, a judgment based on the assumption that the judge knows what good teaching is and can recognize it when he sees it.

The second point emphasized in our little exercise is that we usually evaluate the technician—plumber, auto mechanic, television repairman—on the basis of the results he produces; but that we do not judge the professional—physician, dentist, lawyer—this way.

There seems to be general though tacit agreement that the appropriate basis for evaluating a physician (or any other professional) is whether he follows what is agreed upon, either on the basis of research or professional judgment, as the *best practice* in a given circumstance. We recognize that many influences other than the physician's skill in diagnosis and treatment—the nature of the illness, how far advanced it is, the health, age, vitality, and lifestyle of the patient, his willingness to follow the physician's instructions—will determine the outcome of an individual case. It obviously would be unfair to evaluate the individual physician on the basis of the outcomes he achieves when so much of what determines those outcomes is beyond his control.

When we are comparing the effectiveness of different treatments, however, it is appropriate and necessary to base the comparison on outcomes. When competing treatments are applied by large numbers of physicians to large numbers of patients, those variables that cannot be controlled have an opportunity to even out in comparisons between treatments. This is, of course, how best practice is usually determined. Once a finding has been established in this way and made part of the knowledge of the field, then it becomes the responsibility of the physician to know the finding and to know when and how to apply it. It is then appropriate to evaluate him on the basis of whether the treatment he uses in any one case is the most appropriate one based on current knowledge in the field. Such an evaluation is rare but when it is done it is done carefully, and by other physicians.

The problems confronted by the technician are likely to be much less complex than those encountered by the professional; most or all of them will have known solutions, so that if the diagnosis is accurately made the outcome of treatment can be predicted with a high degree of success. The difference in the problems they are expected to solve is the critical difference between professional and nonprofessional practitioners.

This difference is accompanied by a difference in our expectations of the two kinds of practitioners. If you take your television set to the repairman and he judges it to be beyond repair, you expect him to tell you so and do nothing. But if you take your mother to a physician and he judges her to have terminal cancer, you expect him to tell you so, and to provide her with the best possible care until the end. You neither expect nor want the technician to treat cases in which there is no assurance of success, but you do expect the professional to treat all cases regardless of probable outcome. It would be manifestly unfair, then, to evaluate him by the outcome he gets. The mortality rate for the physician who regularly treats serious heart disease or cancer cases is expected to exceed that for the family physician who rarely meets such serious problems. And are there not some teaching situations in which it is much more difficult to succeed than in others? Most would agree that this is the case.

The point of view which will be taken in this volume is that today's teachers must be evaluated as professionals, not as technicians, because we demand that they teach every child and that they offer him the best possible chance to learn, regardless of how easy or difficult that may be. Just as the best physician may fail to cure some patients, so the best teacher will fail to teach some pupils; but the responsibility of both is the same, that of using the best practice available at the time.

Since today's teacher is not a technician who needs to deal only with problems that have known solutions she can neither be held responsible for nor evaluated on the basis of the results she gets. The teacher of a few generations ago may indeed have functioned as a technician rather than as a professional. In those days, we understand, pupils who did not find the traditional style of teaching congenial, who were difficult to teach by methods then available, soon dropped out of school, until the only pupils left were the ones whom the teacher was able to teach successfully. Education was viewed as a privilege available only to those who could benefit from it, and failures were usually blamed on deficiencies in pupil motivation or learning ability rather than deficiencies in teaching skill.

If this was indeed true then, it certainly is not true today. Now every pupil who comes through the classroom door must stay and must learn, because some legislative or judicial mandate says he must. According to Wise (1979), if a pupil fails to learn, his teacher may be violating a law and therefore committing a crime.

Until the middle of the present century, such research in teaching as there was was not concerned with identifying best practice but with identifying personal qualities widely believed to distinguish more effective from less effective teachers. These characteristics were identified by asking people the same questions that we asked at the beginning of this chapter; in this way it was found that more effective teachers were brighter, better informed about subject matter, conveyed a different sense of presence, had different attitudes, values, or personality characteristics, etc., than less effective ones. This information led to the development and use of scales for rating teachers on personal characteristics such as grooming, punctuality, warmth, congeniality, etc. Lore of this kind made up what we "knew" about effective teaching; much of it persists today, and many teacher educators are strongly committed to these plausible but empirically unsubstantiated beliefs.

An illustration of the consequences of this commitment to what we "know" occurred in the recent experience of one of the authors. As so often occurs, a first-year teacher was hired to teach a class of disadvantaged junior high students; that is, she was assigned to the most difficult teaching situation in the grade. The year got off to a bad start and went down hill from there. As the teacher struggled to establish the kind of classroom she felt would be desirable, the idea occurred to her that perhaps she didn't "look like a teacher"—wasn't as well groomed as effective teachers are—and that if she improved her personal appearance things might go better in the classroom. So she began coming to school in her Sunday best. But it didn't help, and things continued to get worse. Instead of giving up, she tried something else; she sought help from one of her colleagues who happened to pay more attention to the research findings on classroom management than to the folklore of teaching. The colleague was able to suggest a more effective set of procedures, which the new teacher applied. Conditions began to improve in her classroom, and she finished the year an enthusiastic and successful young teacher. She did so not by changing her personal characteristics, but by changing what she *did* in the classroom.

This book was written in the belief that the characteristics of the teacher that are important are those that are visible in her classroom behavior. This view has one great advantage: the characteristics with which we will be concerned are ones which we can observe, evaluate, and do something about. Research that tells us whether students learn more from blue-eyed teachers than from brown-eyed ones might be useful in screening candidates for admission to teacher education programs; but it would be of no help to us in understanding the nature of effective teaching or in helping teachers become more effective. If we evaluate teachers mainly to improve teaching, we would hardly want to do so on the basis of eye color.

EVALUATING TEACHERS BY CLASSROOM BEHAVIOR

What we have said thus far indicates that it is inappropriate to evaluate teachers either on the basis of outcomes or of personal characteristics, and suggests instead that we should evaluate them on the basis of their performance—their classroom behavior. Some of you might believe that modern teacher rating instruments do not rate teachers on personal characteristics. What a modern rating scale tries to do is to locate a classroom on a scale from one to five on a dimension of classroom behavior, such as orderly to disorderly, warm to cold, permissive to nonpermissive, or effective to ineffective. But neither past experience nor research offers much support for this procedure because teachers rated high on these dimensions do not typically produce greater pupil learning gains than teachers rated low on them. If we drew a number between one and five from a hat, that number would predict teacher effectiveness almost as well as one of these ratings, as far as we can tell.

According to research based on rating instruments, the widespread use of such ratings in efforts to improve the quality of teachers may be expected to have no effect. Whether they are used to decide which teachers should be certified, hired, given tenure, awarded merit increases, or given in-service training, drawing names from a hat should be just about as effective. The continuing allegations that too many incompetent teachers are being trained, certified, hired, and given tenure may be true; if so, they are consistent with what research tells us.

There are two possible reasons why ratings of teachers made by experts lack validity. One is that they may be rating the wrong things, that the dimensions they rate are irrelevant to teacher effectiveness. The other is that the procedure itself may be ineffective, may be too crude and insensitive or have other limitations that make it intrinsically invalid.

Let us consider the first explanation briefly. Do we know enough about which dimensions of classroom performance relate to teacher effectiveness to enable us to develop valid rating scales (if such thing is possible)? Knowledge about the nature of effective teaching comes from three sources which differ in their levels of credibility. At the highest level is information that comes from *empirical research* that is sound in design and generalizability. Such knowledge is not infallible, but the risk that it will eventually turn out to be false is small. At the second level is knowledge that comes from *theory*. Theories extend knowledge derived from research on logical grounds. Theoretical knowledge is consistent with research but not established by it. We expect that most of it will eventually be confirmed by research. At the third level is knowledge that comes from *clinical experience*, that is, from the experiences of practitioners, but which has not yet been verified by research. In our generous moods we refer to this as conventional wisdom; in our less generous moods we call it the folklore of the profession.

Someone has said that the purpose of research is to find out what part of what we know (from the conventional wisdom) is true, and what part is false. Such research as there is on this point—which is by no means definitive—suggests that about half of what we know is true and half is false. It is critical to note that rating scales are based on both halves, and this fact is sufficient in itself to explain why they lack validity.

The amount of Level 1 knowledge we have today about effective teaching is substantially greater than it was 20 years ago, but is still insufficient to serve as a complete basis for defining enough dimensions of effective teaching for an adequate teacher evaluation system. It is therefore necessary to draw on the less dependable knowledge at Level 2, and perhaps even Level 3.

We do not mean to suggest, nor do we believe, that because research-based knowledge is incomplete we should not use it. One popular way of dealing with any proposed change in what we are used to doing is to compare the effects of the change with an ideal, and abandon the change if it falls short of the ideal. Since it always does, this is an excellent way of preserving the status quo ante. While we are waiting for the definitive results of research to come in, we can go on doing whatever we think best.

An alternative strategy is the one recommended, and followed by Sir Robert Watson-Watt, the man who is credited with the invention of radar, who said, "Give them the third-best to go on. The best never comes, and the second-best comes too late" (Schutz, 1974). The strategy we recommend is to compare the results expected from the change with the way things are, and adopt the change if the evidence indicates it is better then what we are doing now. Let us use all the research-based knowledge we have, and then patch up the gaps as best we can.

This book was written because we feel that no matter how completely and correctly we are able to define the dimensions of effective teaching, we will never be able to evaluate teaching adequately with rating scales. It is the purpose of this book to describe an alternative to rating based on structured observations which can yield valid evaluations of teaching once the important dimensions have become known. And, perhaps more importantly, it can help us, as it already has, to develop the knowledge itself.

The experience of researchers in teacher effectiveness, who have tried to develop this kind of knowledge, is highly relevant. Such research began almost a hundred years ago, and by mid-century the literature it generated contained more than a thousand entries (Domas and Tiedeman, 1951). No useful findings could be gleaned from all this literature, however. Not long after, there was a radical change in such research: researchers abandoned the rating scale and began to use structured observation schedules. They began to produce results almost immediately. In a review of 14 studies done in the 1960s and 1970s, chosen for the soundness of their design, we found more than 600 significant relationships between classroom behavior and pupil learning gains, including a substantial number whose generalizability had been established by being replicated in independent studies (Medley, 1977). (See Appendix A.) Those phenomena clearly indicate that structured observation systems can identify and measure important dimensions of teacher performance—dimensions that are clearly related to how effective the teacher is in producing pupil learning gains.

It is time that those of us who are responsible for evaluating individual teachers as a basis for decisions about certification, training, or employment followed the example of the researchers and abandoned the rating scales we have used essentially unchanged for over 70 years, in favor of structured observation systems similar to those the researchers have used so effectively. As you read over our descriptions of how you should proceed in making this important transition, it may seem to be so difficult a task that you will be tempted to stick with the rating scales. Rather than do that, we recommend that you start out in a relatively small way at first and then, after you discover for yourself the impact you can have, expand the program gradually.

One of the most visible and acute problems some teachers have is that of establishing and maintaining a classroom environment that is favorable to learning. Most visible, not only to the school staff but to parents as well, is the teacher's success in maintaining order in the classroom. The annual surveys of parent concerns conducted by Gallup for *Phi Delta Kappan* magazine (1982) invariably find this one high on the list. Then there are some teachers who maintain order, but do so by creating a tense, punitive environment scarcely any more favorable to learning than a disorderly one.

There will be relatively few teachers in any school who feel that the environment in their classroom could not be improved in some way. This is an area in which there is both a useful amount of Level 1 knowledge to help teachers improve and instrumentation readily adoptable to use for teacher evaluation. (See Appendix E.) What we suggest is that you begin by identifying improvement of the learning environment as a staff development goal for a year, and adopt one of these existing instruments as a means for defining and measuring the classroom environment. Evaluations can be made early in the year which will diagnose areas of weaknesses on which each teacher can focus her efforts to improve. A system of support can be set up to help teachers change their behavior. Evaluations made later in the year can confidently be expected to detect substantial progress, but chances are the improvement will be visible to all concerned.

Once this has been done, you will be ready to define other dimensions of teaching and work for improvement in them. They will be more difficult to define, evaluate, and change; you will find less help in the research literature with any of these tasks. You may feel that it is important to validate what you are doing by relating your evaluations to measures of pupil learning and find yourself doing your own research on the side.

In the pages that follow we will try to provide as much help as we can in all phases of the process. Chapter 2 is devoted to defining the *process of teacher evaluation* and its basis, and to defining terms. *Preexisting teacher characteristics* are personal qualities of the teacher (such as general intelligence) which should be assessed before admission to professional training. *Teacher competencies* are specific knowledges, skills, or value positions (such as the ability to ask higher-order questions) believed to be related to teacher effectiveness; *competence* is the repertoire of competencies a teacher possesses. Teacher competence should be assessed before the teacher is certified or hired, and used as a basis for decisions about further training. *Teacher performance* refers to the behavior of the teacher while teaching (such as how many questions she asks). It should be recorded and evaluated before a teacher receives tenure or merit pay. *Pupil learning experiences* are activities believed to promote pupil learning (such as reading aloud) which the teacher arranges for her pupils. They have not so far been used as a basis for teacher evaluation. *Teacher effectiveness* is defined in terms of the scores the teachers' pupils earn on tests or inventories.

The focus of this book is on evaluating *teacher performance*. There are four necessary steps in the process: defining the task to be performed, securing a permanent record of the teacher's behavior while performing it, scoring the record, and comparing the score (or scores) with a standard (or set of standards).

Chapter 3 will examine the *state of the art of teacher evaluation*, focusing on three main approaches: competency testing and other measures of teacher characteristics, measurement of pupil learning gains, and rating teacher performance. The lack of any appreciable amount of evidence that any of the three is valid or reliable for the purpose of teacher evaluation, and reasons for this lack, are discussed.

Chapter 4 deals with the problem of *deciding what behaviors will be observed and recorded*, on whose frequency of occurrence the evaluations will be based. The use of general beliefs about good teaching (Level 3 knowledge); of theoretical formulations of competent teaching (Level 2 knowledge); and of empirical findings (Level 1 knowledge) will be discussed. A set of tables which provide access to the results of research in teacher effectiveness is introduced.

Chapter 5 describes the three principal *types of structured observation systems* developed and used by researchers, with examples of each. Category systems, sign systems, and multiple coding systems are reviewed. Finally, a few notes on the construction of an observation schedule are presented.

Chapter 6 deals with the problems of *defining the task* the teacher is to perform in relationship to the level of competence to be evaluated. Procedures for defining the strategy or plan the teacher is following and the internal and external context in which she works will be described and evaluated.

Chapter 7 is concerned with *obtaining a record* of teacher performance that is objective and accurate, and with such things as the selection and training of observers and their deployment in the field.

Chapter 8 has to do with *scoring the record*—that is, with developing and refining the procedure by which a score, or set of scores, is to be derived from a record. Initially, scoring keys are developed in advance from knowledge at one or more of the three levels already defined. Such keys constitute operational definitions of dimensions of teacher performance. When a set of records is scored on the keys it becomes possible to analyze the scores, revise the definitions, and refine the keys to conform more closely to the realities of teaching.

Chapter 9 will contain suggestions for exploiting the strengths of measurement-based teacher evaluation. One of the oddest facts about public education today is the paucity of information available to decision makers about what is going on in the classrooms. Teachers rarely have any direct knowledge about what happens in classrooms other than their own; and other school personnel are no better informed. Records are kept of everything from pupils' test scores to the number of books circulated in the library; but no records are kept of the events for which the school exists: what happens while pupils are actually being taught. Such knowledge would seem to be essential to assessing need for change, planning and implementing programs for change, and determining whether change occurs.

Implementation of a program of measurement-based teacher evaluation provides as a by-product regular systematic documentary records of events in the classrooms, records which have many potential uses besides the one for which they are obtained. One such use is to provide objective feedback to the teacher about what is going on in her own class.

If the scoring keys are developed in consultation with the teachers, as they normally would be, they provide a clear understanding of the school's goals for the staff development program and point the way to achieve them.

Every teacher knows that when a motivated pupil studies, what he studies is determined by what he thinks will be on the final examination, and that when a motivated teacher teaches, what she does is determined by her perception of the objectives of the course. The process works best when the two perceptions coincide: when the pupil is trying to learn what the teacher is trying to teach. The same principle operates when a teacher is trying to benefit from a staff development program. The closer the agreement between her perception of the basis of performance evaluation and the actual objectives of the program, the greater her progress will be. Clarification of objectives may be one of the most important qualities of a measurement-based system of teacher evaluation.

Such clarity is possible only if the evaluations are specific, behavioral and objective, and only if a teacher's evaluation does not depend on anyone's opinion (however expert) but on her behavior alone. If for no other reason, measurement-based teacher evaluation should replace teacher rating because it approaches this desirable state of affairs so much more closely.

Finally, let us emphasize what must by now be obvious: what we are describing is not an easier way to evaluate teacher performance but a better way. There is no easy solution to this complex and difficult problem; but there is a solution which, though difficult, is perfectly feasible. You must decide whether the solution is important enough to justify the trouble.

BIBLIOGRAPHY

Domas, S. J., and D. V. Tiedeman. "Teacher Competence: An Annotated Bibliography." *Journal of Experimental Education*, 1951, *19*, 103–218.

Gallup, George H. "The 14th Annual Gallup Poll of the Public's Attitudes toward the Public Schools." *Phi Delta Kappan*, September, 1982, 37–50.

Medley, Donald M. *Teacher Competence and Teacher Effectiveness, A Review of Process-Product Research*. Washington, DC: American Association of Colleges for Teacher Education, 1977.

Schutz, Richard E. "What We Say We Don't Know Is Hurting Us." *Educational Researcher*, December, 1974, 3 (11).

Wise, Arthur E. *Legislated Learning: The Bureaucratization of the American Classroom*. Berkeley, CA: University of California Press, 1979.

2

Measurement-Based Teacher Evaluation

Before we embark on any important undertaking, it is important to make sure we know exactly what we propose to do, why we propose to do it, and the best way to go about it. Before we begin the important undertaking of evaluating teacher performance in particular, we need to make sure we understand the process of teacher evaluation, why we intend to evaluate the teacher, and exactly what purpose we wish to accomplish by doing the evaluation. It is particularly important that we have a clear concept of what we propose to do, of the nature of the evaluation process itself; the elucidation of the nature of this process will be the main business of this chapter.

You should not be put off by the fact that the discussion to follow will be somewhat abstract, or that its meaning may not become fully clear to you on first reading. The rest of this book will be devoted to applying the abstract principles to the specifics of the evaluation of teaching.

There are four terms that are widely used, often interchangably, in discussions of teacher evaluation which we wish to distinguish clearly from one another throughout this volume. The terms are:

- *Teacher competency*, a specific knowledge, ability, or value position that a teacher either possesses or does not possess, which is believed to be important to success as a teacher.
- *Teacher competence*, the repertoire of competencies a teacher

14

possesses. The more competencies a teacher possesses the more competent the teacher is said to be.

- *Teacher performance*, what the teacher does on the job; it is defined in terms of teacher behavior under a specified set of conditions. How well a teacher performs depends in part on how competent the teacher is—what competencies the teacher possesses—and in part on the situation in which the teacher performs.
- *Teacher effectiveness*, the results a teacher gets; it is defined in terms of what pupils do, not what the teacher does or can do.

We shall have a good deal more to say about these four terms and will define them more fully in the pages to come; the distinctions we have made among them are critical to our understanding of the process of teacher evaluation. This chapter will be devoted largely to clarifying the differences between these terms and spelling out the implications of the differences for teacher evaluation. We shall first discuss the various points at which teachers have been or might be evaluated, the dimensions of teaching accessible at each point, and the logical interrelationships among the dimensions. Next we shall discuss the essential elements or steps in the objective evaluation of human performance, with particular regard to how these matters bear on the problem of evaluating teacher performance.

THE DYNAMICS OF TEACHER EVALUATION

There are five important points in the professional career of a teacher at which teachers may be and have been evaluated for various purposes and in terms of various dimensions of teaching. These five points are shown schematically in Figure 2.1 together with some other factors which have major effects on teaching.

The first point shown in the diagram is the point at which a candidate applies for formal admission to professional preparation, or in some other way identifies with the teaching profession. We shall refer to the qualities of the candidate that are accessible to evaluation at this point as *preexisting personal characteristics* of the teacher. They include those abilities, knowledges, and values which the entering candidate should already possess and is therefore not expected to acquire as a part of professional teacher education.

When a candidate completes her preservice preparation it is customary and appropriate to assess her *competence*, that is, to determine what competencies—skills, knowledges, and values—she possesses at that point. It is appropriate at this point to ascertain whether or not the

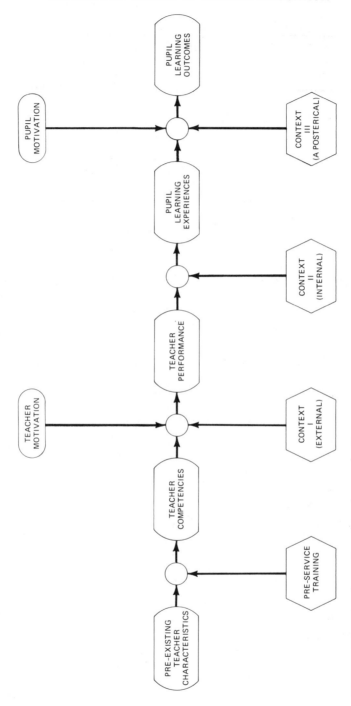

FIGURE 2.1 The dynamics of teacher evaluation.

candidate is competent to practice the teaching profession; that is, can practice it without detriment to the pupils entrusted to her care.

When the candidate has accepted a position as a teacher in a school it becomes appropriate to evaluate the teacher's *performance* of that job; that is, to evaluate how successfully the teacher deploys her competencies in that situation.

In the process of education, the central function of the teacher is to provide pupils with classroom experiences that will result in their learning the things education is designed to teach them. Teaching may therefore be evaluated on the basis of the *pupil learning experiences* that the teacher provides.

Finally, we may evaluate a teacher on the basis of the *learning outcomes* she produces; that is, those changes in pupils which persist after the teaching is over that are attributable to the efforts of the teacher.

Clear distinctions among these points are essential to effective teacher evaluation. There is one and only one point at which evaluations made for any given purpose can be made most effectively. This principle does not seem to be understood by everyone who evaluates teachers; at least it is often violated in practice.

Evaluating Preexisting Personal Characteristics of Teachers.   The point of entry into professional teacher education is the point at which we should find out whether, given a reasonable amount of professional preparation, a would-be teacher can be trained to be a competent teacher. The most obvious purpose of evaluations made at this point is to decide whether or not an individual candidate should be admitted to preservice teacher education.

It is generally assumed that there are certain characteristics which a person must possess in order to be successful as a teacher—patience, perhaps, or a certain kind of interpersonal sensitivity. If so, here is the point in the candidate's career at which these characteristics should be evaluated. It is also generally accepted that there are certain characteristics, such as academic ability, that a person must possess in order to complete successfully a course of professional preparation. These should also be assessed on entry. Unless we think we can teach a candidate to be patient, to be sensitive to the needs and feelings of others, and increase her academic ability, we owe it to candidates to make certain they possess these qualities before we admit them to teacher education.

This is also the appropriate point at which to assess those knowledges, skills, and values that a candidate needs but is expected to have acquired elsewhere. Basic literacy, certain communication skills, and a general liberal education are examples of characteristics which a student should have acquired before she begins professional training. For instance, a student who has not learned to communicate orally by the time she applies for teacher training (usually in the third year of college) is not likely ever to acquire that skill. Certainly training in so basic a skill should form no part of the professional curriculum.

The problem of identifying which preexisting personal characteristics a candidate should be required to possess before she can be admitted to a professional teacher education program remains largely unsolved. Much past research into the problem has sought to correlate preexisting teacher characteristics either with performance on the job or with pupil learning outcomes., The rationale for such research is sound enough; but—as a glance at Figure 2.1 makes clear—the chances of detecting such correlations is slight indeed, because of the number of other variables that intervene and attenuate the correlations sought.

It would be much more useful to look for correlations between preexisting characteristics (such as academic ability) necessary for successful completion of professional preparation and competencies (measured at the end of preservice preparation).

Preexisting characteristics important to success in teaching (such as patience or general literacy) can be identified by correlating measurements of the degree to which practicing teachers possess them with measurements of their teaching performance. Such concurrent correlational studies are much more likely to pay off than the longitudinal studies done in the past.

Evaluating Teacher Competence. The appropriate use of evaluations of teacher competence is as a basis for deciding whether or not a teacher education student should be admitted to the practice of teaching. If we follow the precedents set by other professions, we will base this decision on whether the candidate possesses the minimum set of competencies believed necessary to the safe practice of the profession. By *safe practice* we mean practice that will not be detrimental to the patient, the client, or (in this case) the pupil.

It is well recognized by other professions that none of their members are fully competent when they first enter practice: full competence is achieved (if ever) only after extensive experience in actual practice. Most of what a professional needs to know can only be learned on the job—that is why we say that she or he *practices* a profession. Preservice professional education can at best only prepare the candidate to begin this process, can only give him or her enough professional knowledge, basic professional skill, and professional values to begin this process of learning—to begin to practice—and avoid malpractice, which might harm or injure the recepients of the professional services.

Research that identifies the minimal competencies that a beginning teacher needs in order to practice safely should provide the knowledge base for preservice teacher education. Such research would intercorrelate measures of teacher competence at the point of entry into practice with measures of performance of first-year teachers, with statistical or experimental controls on *external context* or *Type I* context variables; that is, on the type and level of support provided to the teacher in the setting in which she is employed.

Research in teacher effectiveness, including process-product research has in general sought intercorrelations between measures of teacher performance and teacher effectiveness (rather than between teacher competencies and teacher performance). Such research does not shed much direct light on the question that concerns us here, that of minimum competence, and cannot therefore provide a satisfactory research base for preservice teacher education.

A certificate of competence to practice the teaching profession should not be viewed as a guarantee that its possessor will perform successfully in any particular job situation. There are many reasons why a competent teacher may fail to perform satisfactorily on the job. Certification is designed to protect the public only from failures due to lack of minimal competence, that is, to inadequate preparation. It is the responsibility of the school administration to protect the public from failures due to other factors (such as inadequate support); meeting this responsibility depends on evaluation of *performance* rather than of competence.

Evaluating Teacher Performance.   Evaluation of teachers at this, the third point in Figure 2.1, focuses on the teaching act itself. Performance evaluation is designed to evaluate the teacher on the basis of the quality of teaching she provides in a specific setting—with a particular class, in a particular school, in a particular community. It is, of course, process based—based on the behavior of the teacher in the setting.

The problem of measuring teacher performance lies at the very heart of the problem of teacher evaluation. *Teacher performance* refers, of course, to the actual behavior of the teacher while she is in her classroom with her class, not to the effects her behavior has on the pupils. The competencies and other characteristics that a teacher possesses must not be confused with her performance on the job. They affect teacher performance and may in some cases be inferred from it; but they are not the same thing. The effects that the teacher has on the pupils—whether on the experiences they have in school or on the learnings they retain afterward—depend on the performance, but are not the same.

It is not surprising, then, that almost all teacher evaluation is based on teacher performance. This is true regardless of the use to be made of the evaluations. Most decisions about the utilization of teacher personnel in the schools, including decisions related to hiring, promotion, rewards for merit, tenure, or termination of employment, are so based. It is entirely logical to base such decisions on teacher performance—on how the teacher behaves when she is doing, or attempting to do, the job she was engaged to do.

Performance assessments are sometimes used to make decisions for which they are somewhat less directly suitable. For example, teacher performance assessments are sometimes used to decide whether an individual teacher needs further training, and to plan in-service training for a teacher or a group of teachers. Such decisions as these should be based on measures of competence rather than performance. The implied assumption that any deficiencies in performance detected are due to a lack of some competency (or set of competencies) on the part of the teacher may or may not be true. Competencies can only be inferred from performance; but they cannot be assessed directly by measuring on-the-job behavior because many important factors (of which the competence of the teacher is just one) combine to affect the behavior of a teacher in the classroom. These are represented in the figure as *Type I* or *external* context variables.

The validity of evaluations of teacher performance depends on firm knowledge of the nature of optimal performance (best practice). This is the kind of knowledge that process-product research is designed to produce. When teacher performance is correlated with its effects on pupils, it is important to take account of context variables because what is optimal performance may vary from situation to situation

Evaluating Pupil Learning Experiences.   The primary role or function of the teacher in the educational process is to provide pupils with experiences which result in the pupils' learning the things that education is designed to teach them. To state that learning is something the pupil himself must do, that how a pupil behaves determines what the pupil learns, is to state the obvious. It is equally obvious that teacher performance is important or successful only to the degree that it produces pupil learning. Since any effect teaching has on pupil learning depends on how it affects pupil behavior, that is, on the experiences pupils have as a result of the teaching, it seems logical to evaluate teaching on the basis of the experiences it provides for pupils.

Although we all know these things, most of us tend to think of teaching mainly as a process by which a teacher communicates knowledge to pupils, and in planning or evaluating instruction we tend to pay more attention to what the teacher is supposed to do than on what the pupils ought to do.

Assessment of pupil learning experiences might seem, then, to be a more direct and cogent basis for evaluating teaching than assessment of teaching performance itself, since it contains direct information about how well the teacher succeeds in performing the central function of teaching. This is neither an accurate conclusion to reach nor a particularly useful one.

First of all, there are many factors beside the behavior of the teacher which affect the pupils' behavior; as a result, the quality of pupil learning experiences may not reflect the quality of teacher performance very accurately unless these factors are taken into account. Factors that relate to the characteristics of the pupils in the class are of particular importance. They may be referred to as *Type II* context variables or as elements in the *internal context* in which the teaching takes place.

It should be obvious that pupils who receive essentially identical treatment from the teacher may or may not have identical learning experiences: individual pupils respond to teachers differently. One technique of motivation turns some pupils on; a different technique works with others. There may be several ways of maintaining pupil involvement which work equally well with a given pupil or group of pupils. We do not expect identical teaching performances to produce identical pupil behavior in different classes or in the same class at different times because of variations in internal context. This is why it is important to distinguish the performance of the teacher from the experiences of the pupils and to assess them separately.

In the last section we noted that it was possible to infer whether a teacher possessed a certain competency or not from the way the teacher behaved while teaching—from the way the teacher performed. We saw that such a thing was possible but difficult. However, it is *not* possible to make dependable inferences about whether or not a teacher possesses a specific competency from the behavior of the teacher's pupils. Measures of pupil behavior do not contain the diagnostic information, the information about how the teacher behaved, that is necessary for such inferences. Such measures indicate how well, but not *how* the teacher performed.

Measures of pupil learning experiences are in fact measures of teacher effectiveness, not of teaching performance or teacher competence. Such measures could be useful in making personnel decisions; a teacher who cannot successfully perform her central function in a setting—who cannot get pupils to do the things they need to do in order to learn—should not be employed to work in that setting, no matter how competent she may be, or how satisfactory her teaching performance may appear to an observer.

The validity of such evaluations would depend on reliable knowledge about the relationships between pupil learning experiences and pupil outcomes. Knowledge of how pupils learn in school, of what pupil experiences are optimal, would seem to be a central part of the knowledge competencies teachers should acquire in their professional training.

Evaluating Teaching Outcomes.   The fifth and final point at which teacher evaluation might take place is at the level of *pupil learning outcomes.* That is to say, we might evaluate teaching on the basis of changes in pupils that persist after the teaching is over. Since the production of such changes is the ultimate purpose of education, that is the bottom line, the final or criterion measure of the quality of teaching.

However, the number and the potency of the contextual factors not under the teacher's control that affect pupil learning outcomes are both so great that valid measures of the effectiveness of individual teachers are extremely difficult and costly to obtain from pupil outcome data. In addition to contextual variables of Types I and II, there is a third type of context variables which affects outcomes, *Type III.* These factors account for the fact that pupils who have identical learning experiences often do not show identical outcomes. There are other difficulties in evaluating teacher effectiveness as well; we shall discuss some of them in a later chapter.

Review of the Dynamics of Teacher Evaluation

In the foregoing pages we have seen that teacher evaluations may be made at any one of five points in a teacher's career: (1) on entry into preservice preparation; (2) on completion of preservice preparation and before entry into practice; (3) on the basis of the teacher's behavior while teaching; (4) on the basis of the pupils' behavior during teaching; (5) on the basis of learning outcomes.

It seems clear that at the first two points we are evaluating personal qualities of the teacher which are retained in any situation in which she may be employed. It also seems clear that since assessments made at the last two points are based on the behavior of pupils rather than teachers, they do not measure anything about the teacher directly.

The third point is the central point, the point at which whatever qualities the teacher may possess affect the behaviors of the pupils. This is the main point at which we evaluate teaching and teachers; it is the point at which teaching occurs. Evaluations made at this point are properly called evaluations of *teacher performance.*

Sometimes our interest lies not in the performance that we are measuring, but elsewhere—for some purposes we are interested in inferring the *effectiveness* of the teacher from her performance; for others we may be interested in inferring the teacher's *competence* from her performance.

It would appear that improvement of teaching, and its effects on pupils, can be achieved in three ways: (1) by improving the teacher, (2) by improving the situation, or (3) by using both more efficiently without changing either. The first method depends on increasing teacher competence; the second depends on such actions as improving physical facilities or instructional materials, restructuring classes, etc. The third seems to depend on teacher morale and motivation.

Effective use of any one of the three approaches requires accurate evaluations of teacher performance; but it also requires accurate information about the other factors as well, if an intelligent decision is to be made about which approach to adopt. In-service training can improve teaching only if a lack of competence is what is causing the problem in the first place. To know that the quality of teaching in a classroom is low is to know that a problem exists; solving the problem requires knowing the reason.

THE STRUCTURE OF PERFORMANCE EVALUATION

The process of performance evaluation involves four segments or steps; objective performance evaluation requires that each step be performed with a high degree of objectivity. The key is isolating each step from the others. The four steps are:

1. Setting, defining, or agreeing upon a *task* to be performed.
2. Making a documentary, quantifiable *record* of the behavior of the candidate while the task is performed.
3. Quantifying the record, that is, deriving a *score* or set of scores from it.
4. Comparing the scores with the predetermined *standard*.

We shall now discuss the purpose and rationale for each of the four steps and how each fits into the process of evaluation of teacher performance. Ways and means, dos and don'ts, and the like will be discussed in subsequent chapters.

Step 1: Defining the Task

Since teaching performance is purposeful, the purpose of any sample of teaching performance must be known, any attempt to evaluate the performance must be done in relationship to that purpose.

Evaluation may be thought of in simple terms as a matter of discriminating "good" from "bad," what is valued from what is not valued. Whether a particular behavior or behavior pattern is good or not depends on whether it is appropriate to whatever purpose the performer is trying to accomplish. Asking a higher-order question, praising a pupil response, rebuking a pupil—whether any one of these behaviors is appropriate at any particular time depends on what the teacher is trying to accomplish and, to a less but important extent, on how she plans to accomplish it. None of these actions is intrinsically good or bad, appropriate or inappropriate. Each one may be bad at one time and good at another. The definition of the task that a teacher is trying to perform is important primarily as *a basis for identifying appropriate and inappropriate behaviors*. This makes evaluating the performance possible.

The definition has another critically important function. We need to select or agree on tasks in such a way that in performing them the teacher who can do so will display mastery of those competencies (knowledges, skills, attitudes) that characterize the performance of an effective teacher in each situation. A candidate who can perform effectively may fail to do so if she misinterprets the task definition and tries to perform some other task, for which different behaviors are appropriate, and our evaluation will be incorrect. This second reason why defining the task is important may be phrased as *to ensure that a candidate who can do so will perform the task successfully*.

A third reason why defining the task is essential is *to make it possible to compare performances* by ensuring that all teachers will try to perform the same task, or (when that is impractical) comparable tasks. Only then will differences in performances reflect differences in teachers rather than in tasks.

We are aware that some educators regard comparisons as odious. One manifestation of this point of view is the current popularity of criterion-referenced tests, which purport to measure performance in absolute terms without employing inter-individual comparisons. Such absolute measurements are useless, however, unless comparisons of some sort are used, consciously or unconsciously. Evaluation has to do with "good" and "bad," two entities we cannot define operationally. What we can define are the related terms "better" and "worse"; these are the ones that govern decisions in the real world, including those necessary to define performance standards. Decisions based on teacher evaluations are no exception; defining equivalent tasks is essential if such decisions are to be valid.

To secure a sample of performance of comparable and relevant tasks, and to provide a basis for scoring the performances—the reasons why arriving at a clear task definition, a clear agreement between the teacher and the evaluator about the purpose of the performance—is a necessary step in the process of measurement-based evaluation of teacher performance.

Step 2: Obtaining the Record

This step is an element often overlooked in the objective evaluation of any performance; but unless we have a record of a performance in scorable form it is not possible to use identical procedures for judging the performances of different candidates. Only a documentary record of a performance can be scored with the same key used to score records of other performances; it makes it possible for us to be sure that similar performances by different teachers will receive similar scores. It makes it possible to eliminate any effects of bias or ignorance on the part of evaluators from comparisons of performance.

How objective an evaluation of teacher performance is depends mainly on how accurate and objective the record is. It is much easier to achieve a high degree of objectivity in records of teacher performance made with a structured observation schedule than in the records of observer judgments obtained with teacher rating scales. This is so mainly because the observer's personal impression or evaluation of a teacher has much less impact on the observational records then on ratings. The experience of researchers using structured observation systems has repeatedly demonstrated that a high level of objectivity and accuracy can be obtained at reasonable cost with such instruments.

A record of a behavior made with such a system contains detailed information about the teacher's performance which has other uses besides providing a basis for scoring the performance. First, such a record contains diagnostic information which is valuable for planning remedial treatment when performance is unsatisfactory. The record indicates precisely how and where the performance fell short, and how the teacher needs to change her behavior in order to achieve satisfactory performance next time.

A set of observational records can be submitted to item analysis, factor analysis, and other statistical procedures that have been developed to improve the validity of objective measurements. As we shall see in Chapter 8, the details in the record also make it possible to study the structure of performance and design better strategies not only for measuring it but for improving it as well. Changes in teacher performance over time can be measured more precisely by comparing before-and-after records than by any other means. And last but not least, if the fairness of an evaluation is challenged in court—if, for example a teacher who fails to be certified sues the certifying agency and accuses it of racial or sexual bias—the record of the performance is available for review. It is possible, for example, to prove from the record that the same criteria were applied to that performance as to those of the teachers who passed, and that the negative evaluation reflects only the performance of the candidate, not some fallible judge's opinion of its quality.

Because the observation schedules or systems list the behaviors to be recorded, they do not require observers to possess any expertise in the teaching process; no expert judgment is involved in recording the behaviors. The skills the observer needs in order to make accurate records with such a schedule can be acquired during a brief period of training. The skills involved are of such a nature that paraprofessional or nonprofessional personnel can master them as quickly and proficiently as professional personnel. By using lower-level staff as observers it is possible to free supervisory, administrative, or other professional staff for duties which capitalize upon their expertise. It is no more necessary to have a principal observe teachers in order to evaluate them than it is for a principal to administer the tests on which the pupils are evaluated. Separating measurement from evaluation and decision making is the key in both cases.

The development (or selection) of an observation system requires you to become very specific and precise in defining the aspects of teacher performance which are relevant to the quality of the performance you wish to evaluate. In all probability you will have to define them more explicitly, operationally, and in greater detail than ever before. This will be a difficult task, but it would seem to be a necessary preliminary to any serious attempt to improve teaching. It is all too easy to overlook this step when you decide to use a rating scale. The experience of making such a specification is likely to have far-reaching (and beneficial) effects on many other activities besides the evaluation of teaching.

Step 3: Scoring the Record

In order to serve the uses we have just listed, records must be made in scorable form. The only way to do this is to use a structured observation system of some kind. A video-taped record of a teacher's performance, for example, may be objective, but it is not in scorable form. Most observation systems in use today yield records made on mark-sensing forms which can be processed mechanically—can be read and scored by machines or clerks. Pocket-sized computers are small enough to be carried into the classroom by observers, and records of behavior can be made by keying coded data directly into them. Such a computer can be programmed to store the record on tape or at times, to score the record immediately. What is essential is that the record be in a form such that the scoring process can be mechanized and can become completely objective.

The weights that will be assigned to specific behaviors in deriving a score from a behavior record are determined and programmed in advance. This is the point at which expert judgment about the teaching-learning process plays its part, when expert judges determine the weights to be used in scoring the records. Thus each performance is in fact rated on the basis of expert judgment; but the same panel of expert judges rate every performance. The scoring key never gets tired or careless, it is absolutely insensitive to such things as race or sex, or any teacher quality not visible in the record.

Scoring a behavior record can be designed to yield a profile of scores just as easily as a single score; in either case, the principles and procedures are essentially the same.

Step 4: Evaluating the Scores

To ensure that the entire process of evaluating teaching is as objective as possible, a standard (or perhaps a set of standards for different purposes) is also specified in advance. The procedure of comparing a candidate's score (or scores) with such a standard can be, and should be, just as objective as any of the other three steps in the evaluation process.

Of course it is possible to make this last step a subjective one, if you wish. If you (or whoever is responsible for doing so) prefer to make up your own mind about a candidate without identifying any standard beforehand, completion of the first three steps as described will provide you with the most accurate, complete, and objective information available on which to base your personal judgment.

Review of the Structure of Performance Evaluation

In this section we have described a model for teacher performance evaluation that is almost perfectly objective. The process involves four steps: (1) defining the task to be performed; (2) obtaining a scorable record of the performance of the task; (3) scoring the record; and (4) comparing the score (or scores) with a standard. Expert judgment enters into the process (1) when the task is defined, (2) when the scoring key is constructed, and (3) when the standard is set. If all of these steps are completed before individual performances are actually evaluated, the expertise will be applied to all records in exactly the same way, preventing any biases from distorting the evaluations.

The objectivity of the procedure is limited mainly by the degree of objectivity achieved in the second step, recording the performance. The use of structured observation makes it feasible to achieve a degree of objectivity that is quite high in comparison to that attainable in any other way.

SUMMARY

In this chapter we have surveyed the domain of teacher evaluation and identified the evaluation of teacher performance on the job as the central focus of this volume. We have also identified four essential steps or phases in the process of evaluating human performance and indicated how they can be applied to the evaluation of teacher performance to maximize its objectivity. In the next chapter we propose to examine some of the procedures currently used in teacher evaluation in the light of what has been said in this chapter.

3

The Inadequacy of the Existing Methods of Teacher Evaluation

In Chapters 1 and 2 we have described an approach to teacher evaluation which we believe the profession must adopt if it is to meet the responsibilities society expects it to meet. Before going into any detail about what the implementation of this approach entails, we propose in this chapter to document the fact that the methods we have used in the past and continue to use in the present are entirely inadequate, and why this is so. It should be clear to the reader that the appropriate target of such evaluation is the competence of the individual teacher: the potential contribution of teacher evaluation to the improvement of education depends on making it possible to identify the most competent teachers in any group of teachers, to diagnose incompetence, and to measure changes in competence validly and reliably.

Existing methods of teacher evaluation have attempted to predict competence from preexisting teacher characteristics, and to assess competence directly through the use of paper-and-pencil tests; they have attempted to infer competence from ratings of teacher performance and from test scores of pupils in the teachers' classes. That these methods have not succeeded is clear from the numbers of incompetent teachers who have found their way into the schools and stayed there until old age forced them to retire. At the time of this writing, state legislatures throughout the country are taking the initiative away from us and are trying to bring about valid evaluation by legislative and judicial mandate. It is difficult to estimate what proportion of the problems of American public education are due to the apparent inability of teacher educators and school administrators to make accurate discriminations between competent and incompetent teachers; but the public and its elected representatives clearly perceive this to be a major factor.

What we have already said should provide some clues as to why we have been unable to discharge this responsibility. In this chapter we propose to examine the experience we have had with the evaluation strategies we have used in the past, of which there have been three. One has been to use paper-and-pencil instruments to measure either pre-existing teacher characteristics (such as intelligence or attitudes toward children) or competencies (mainly knowledge) without making any clear distinction between the two. Another has been to use test scores of pupils in the teacher's class, mainly achievement tests, in an effort to assess learning outcomes. The third, and by far the most common, has been to have experts rate teacher competence or effectiveness on the basis of observations of teacher performance, without making any clear distinction between competence, effectiveness, and performance. Let us briefly and critically review what has happened with each in turn.

PAPER-AND-PENCIL TESTS

In the days when success in teaching was perceived as mainly a function of personal qualities of the teacher rather than of patterns of classroom behavior, at least some of which could be acquired through professional education or training, it seemed logical to try to identify competent teachers in advance by giving them tests of ability, personality, attitudes, etc. For many years an important objective of research on teaching was to identify and measure the characteristics which distinguished good and poor teachers.

That this is no longer so can be verified readily by comparing the original *Handbook of Research on Teaching* (Gage, 1963) with the *Second Handbook of Research on Teaching* (Travers, 1973). In the former, an entire chapter was devoted to a review of research on teacher characteristics; in the latter, not only is there no such chapter, but a search of the index reveals only a few lines on the topic.

Perhaps the best way to get a feel for this research is to reread an exhaustive review and summary which appeared a few years earlier while such research was at its peak (Barr, 1948). One thing that strikes you as you read this most disheartening monograph is that the vast majority of the studies used supervisors' ratings as the criterion of teacher competence; as we shall see, the validity of such a criterion is itself open to question—so much so that no faith can be placed in the findings of such studies.

There were a handful of studies which had used measures of average gains in achievement of pupils in a teacher's class as a criterion. It was the findings of these studies that were most discouraging. The results were highly inconsistent, so that almost any correlation could be matched by another which contradicted it; and the average correlations tended to approach zero. No evidence that a teacher's score on any paper-and-pencil test correlated with her ability to produce pupil gains in achievement was found.

In the early 1940s there appeared a standardized test battery for teachers which is still in existence and in fairly widespread use today called the *National Teacher Examinations* or NTE. The battery includes Area Examinations for teachers in such "areas" as mathematics, art, and so on; but the most widely used portion is the Common Examinations designed to be administered to all teachers. Much more research has been done on this part of the tests; some 40 studies have been reviewed recently (Quirk, Witten, and Weinberg, 1973). Almost all of the research has sought to correlate Weighted Common Examination Total scores with criteria of teacher competence, usually based on ratings but sometimes based on pupil gains on achievement tests. This total is based partly on scores on tests of subject-matter knowledge and partly on tests of professional knowledge. (The publisher of NTE does not recommend the use of scores on individual subtests because they are not reliable enough.)

Once again the results have been uniformly discouraging. There is no evidence that these scores predict success in teaching whether estimated from ratings or from gain scores of pupils.*

One exception should be noted. In a recent study done in North Carolina, a significant correlation was found between the mean NTE scores of teachers hired in a school system and the amount pupils learned in that system (North Carolina Department of Education, 1980). Since most of the pupils involved were not in the new teachers' classes whatever it was that caused pupils in some schools to learn more than those in others could not have been any characteristic of the new teachers relevant to their teaching performance. What seems most likely is that the personnel officer in a more affluent school system pays more attention to NTE scores in choosing teachers than the one in a poor system, and that pupils in the more affluent systems achieve at higher levels.

Concern with the quality of teachers has led a number of states to mandate some kind of a teacher competency test as a basis for teacher certification. The primary concern here has been with so-called teacher illiteracy and ignorance of the content of the school curriculum. As a

---

* Whether or not these findings apply to the revised examinations introduced in 1982 remains to be seen. In view of the nature of the revision, it is our guess that they do.

result, most of these tests are tests of subject-matter knowledge rather than of professional knowledge. Although all efforts to show that scores on such tests are related to effective teaching have failed, we find it difficult to disagree with the general feeling that a teacher should know the subject she teaches. But it appears unwise to expect that the adoption of such teacher competency tests will result in any noticeable improvement in the overall quality of teaching. When a teacher fails for lack of certain competencies, teacher illiteracy and ignorance of school curriculum are rarely the competencies involved. A teacher competent in other ways but weak in knowledge of subject matter can be a far better teacher than one who is a complete master of her subject but lacks other competencies. The ability to create and maintain a wholesome classroom learning environment, the ability to implement effective teaching strategies and involve every child in a class in them—these are the abilities which separate most teachers who succeed from those who do not. And these are the abilities that paper-and-pencil tests fail to measure.

A teacher who cannot pass a test of general literacy, or of the basic skills and knowledge her pupils are supposed to acquire under her tutelage, is one who should never have been admitted to a teacher education program in the first place. It is not and should not be the responsibility of a professional school to teach its students to read and write, to spell and calculate, or to master the basic content of their subject matter fields. These are the objectives of secondary schools and liberal arts colleges; if a college junior interested in preparing to teach has not yet acquired these skills and knowledges, she should not be permitted, much less encouraged, to begin professional study. To permit her to do so, to collect her tuition money for two years and then, after she has completed her courses with passing grades, to deny her certification on these grounds is both wasteful and immoral.

There is also great concern about what to do with teachers now in the field who lack these minimum basic skills. Although we have argued that the measures we advocate should not be used with a teacher who has completed training, that to do so is to penalize the teacher for a mistake made by the program, we agree that any deficiency of the teacher which appears in performance may be an appropriate basis for retraining or possibly for dismissal from employment, if not for decertification. The English teacher who does not dependably put both subject and verb in each sentence as she teaches is clearly not performing competently. Evaluation of the *performance* of a practicing teacher is always appropriate, even though it involves a preexisting teacher characteristic. The fact that a teacher has been certified in no way obligates any school system to employ her unless she does a satisfactory job. A certificate is neither a guarantee of satisfactory performance to the employer nor a guarantee of a job to the teacher.

The validity of paper-and-pencil tests for measuring other kinds of knowledge, including knowledge of how pupils learn and how they may be taught most effectively, has not been established either (cf. Quirk, Witten, and Weinberg, 1973). And there is no evidence (or reason to suppose) that any of them measure or predict the ability to apply either subject matter or professional knowledge in the classroom.

The general conclusion to be drawn is that, although paper-and-pencil tests may have a legitimate role to play in teacher evaluation, they fall far short of meeting our needs as a means for effecting important and visible improvements in classroom teaching.

PUPIL ACHIEVEMENT AS A BASIS FOR EVALUATING TEACHERS

Some have argued that the logical basis for evaluating a teacher is the achievement of her pupils. We reject this attractive notion because of three problems: pupil variability, the regression effect, and the limitations of achievement tests presently available.

Pupil Variability

Advocates of this approach to teacher evaluation argue that if a factory worker's productivity is measured by the number of items he turns out, and that of a salesman by the dollar amount of the sales he closes, why not evaluate a teacher's productivity by the scores her pupils earn on systemwide tests administered at the end of the school year?

The idea is both simple and appealing to the layman. It is an excellent example of what the late H. L. Mencken meant when he noted that every complex problem has a simple, obvious solution which is wrong.

The analogy to the factory worker is a false one, if for no other reason than that the raw material with which he works is of uniform quality, so that the quality of the finished product depends on his efforts alone. The quality of the raw material the teacher works with varies widely; some pupils know more when they enter a grade than the average pupil knows when he leaves it. Some pupils learn only with the greatest difficulty: others learn with ease. Most of the variations in the finished products of teaching were already present in the raw materials, and in no way reflect the competence of the teacher.

The analogy to the salesman also breaks down, mainly on ethical grounds. The salesman works with adults and may—and sometimes does—use means to persuade or entice them that would be unethical if used on children by a teacher. Learning and making a purchase are both acts of free will; when one person is evaluated on the basis of his or her ability to influence what another does, there is a pressure to deceive or compel compliance which may be tolerable in the case of the salesman (although we question it), but would be intolerable in the case of the teacher.

Let us look at some of the factors which make pupils so different. It is well known that one of the strongest influences on a pupil's achievement is his IQ—the intellectual capital available to him to apply to the task of learning. Test manuals commonly report correlations between measures of individual pupils' intelligence or academic aptitude and measures of their achievement ranging from .40 to .70 (depending on grade level). If the correlations are based on class means, as is the case when we evaluate teachers, the correlations between mean achievement and mean pretest and IQ combined may be as high as .90 (Soar and Soar, 1975). This is so because when IQ and a pretest achievement score are combined in this way they tend to reflect most or all of the context factors that affect posttest scores. (Since the pretest score is itself an achievement test score, these factors will already have had a chance to affect the pupil's achievement up to that time.) A correlation of .90 means, of course, that about 80 percent of the differences in the pupil achievement scores used to evaluate a teacher were present before she had any chance to influence them. If the teacher were permitted to choose the pupils she would teach, this would not be so important a factor: but she is not. She is held accountable for these preexisting differences even though she has no control over them!

It is taken for granted that the home is a major influence on pupil learning. Although research on this point is not extensive, there is a modest body of research which supports that belief. Garber and Ware (1972), for example, found a correlation of +.47 between achievement and a measure of support for learning in the home in a group of black and Spanish-American children. Since all of the children in the study met poverty guidelines, the presumably potent influence of socioeconomic status cannot account for this correlation. Findings of other studies (with blacks, with Spanish-American children, and with a number of Indian tribes) parallel these.

Another influence which is widely accepted as powerful, one which may not be reflected in pretest scores, is that of the peer group. The classic work is that of Coleman (1961); more recent is the work of Anderson (1970), who showed that the effect of how closely knit the peer group is varies according to the average ability level of the group. If the group is made up of bright pupils, the closer the involvement between the pupils, the higher their average achievement level; but if the group is made up of low-ability students, the closer the involvement the lower the achievement level. D'Amico (1973) found that among teenage girls, the average achievement level of other members of a clique was a better predictor of the achievement of any one member than her own ability level was. Social influences among students seem to be powerful determiners of their achievement.

If pupils in the same grade, subject, and school building were assigned to classes at random, the variations between classes in the same grade, subject, and school in all such factors as these would be at the chance level; the correlations we have cited would all be zero; and differences in mean end-of-year achievement test scores of different classes would indeed reflect differences in the performances of the teachers. There is nothing inherently difficult about doing this, even when there are certain constraints (political or otherwise) on the assignments. If, for example, there are two or more ethnic groups in the community who must be integrated at the classroom level, or if there are two or more recognized subgroups of pupils in a grade and school with significantly different learning ability, each identified group can be assigned randomly to the classes separately from any other, with the same effect as if all pupils had been randomly assigned as a single group. Even with this procedure, students could not be compared across schools, grades, or subjects.

For some reason, school administrators find it very difficult to randomize, even within such restrictions as we have mentioned. As a result, researchers have evolved statistical procedures designed to achieve the same effect. The basic idea is to use estimates of pupils' *gains* in achievement rather than end-of-year scores to assess the effects of the teacher on pupil achievement. However, obtaining an accurate and unbiased estimate of pupil gains is not a simple matter; none of the procedures generally used (raw gains, residual gains, adjusted mean gains) yields a fully satisfactory measure of teacher effectiveness. Such methods can at best take account only of factors that can be identified and measured, and their effectiveness is further limited by the validities and reliabilities of the tests used.

The best evidence about the effectiveness of these procedures is provided by studies of the stability of the measurements they yield. If the competence of a teacher is to be assessed by a measure of pupil gains in her classes, the measure should be relatively stable from one year to another (or, if the teacher teaches more than one class in the same year, from one class to another).

There are several studies which have estimated stability coefficients of mean gains in a teacher's class as a measure of the competence of the teacher (Rosenshine, 1970; Brophy, 1970). The median value of all such coefficients is around .30. Measurement experts generally agree that any score that is to be used to make decisions about individuals needs a reliability of at least .90 to be usable. This coefficient of .30 falls far short. Using the Spearman-Brown formula, we estimate that the mean of 20 scores with a reliability of .30 would have a reliability of .90; in other words, it would take 20 years to find out whether a teacher is competent or not by this method.

Remember that pupils were not randomly assigned to classes in any of these studies, but that one or another standard procedure supposed to compensate for failure to randomize was used in each case. And yet fully 70 percent of the variations in mean gains were still unaccounted for, reflecting variability of pupils in different classes that the investigators were not able to measure.

If a school system were to use adjusted mean gains of pupils as a technique for evaluating its teachers, that is, if instead of comparing teachers on pupils' standings at the end of the year an effort were made to make allowances for preexisting differences between classes taught by different teachers, more than two-thirds of the differences found would not reflect teacher competence at all. The teacher who had the highest score would be only slightly more likely to be of above-average competence than the one with the lowest. Next year the second teacher would be quite likely to do better than the first.

If the school system evaluated its teachers on end-of-year scores instead of gains, the situation would be much worse; about as accurate as drawing scores out of a hat. Thus, the improvement obtained by using gain scores would be modest indeed.

Deciding which teacher is the best—which to hire, which to fire—by a method that is little better than chance might seem worthwhile for other reasons. To be able to say you are using the best available method, however imperfect, may be politically advantageous. But before deciding to do so it is important to know that the use of the procedure cannot do great harm. If using pupil achievement as a basis for teacher evaluation worked successfully it would probably reduce the quality of teaching instead of improving it.

The Regression Effect

One serious problem that we have not yet mentioned has to do with the *regression effect*, well known to measurement experts but little understood outside that group. Figure 3.1 shows the relation between the pretest and posttest scores for a group of students, ignoring for the moment the average gain made by all pupils. If we mark off the top 10 percent and the bottom 10 percent of fall scores and similarly mark off the top 10 and bottom 10 percent of spring scores, we can see that in a great many cases the students who were in either extreme group in the fall are no longer in that extreme group in the spring. Since this is true, on the average, low-scoring pupils must have moved up relatively between fall and spring and high-scoring pupils must have moved

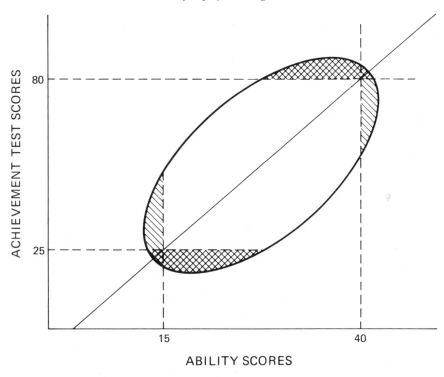

FIGURE 3.1 An illustration of the regression effect.

down. The term *regression effect* comes from the fact that each extreme group tends, on average, to regress toward the mean from one measurement to another. One of our students, colorfully, characterized this as a "Robin Hood effect," since it steals from the rich and gives to the poor.

Although there are a number of explanations which bear on why this phenomenon occurs, perhaps one will suffice. If we think of students who are above the cutoff for the top 10 percent in fall scores, a given student is likely to be in that group because he had a relatively high true score (i.e., he had a relatively high standing in his knowledge of whatever the test measures), but to some degree pupils in that group will also be there because chance happened to fall in their favor on this one test occasion. That is, there will be some students whose true score is near the cutoff but slightly below it, but who got over the cutoff because of chance, on this one occasion. Since chance will be uncorrelated from one occasion to the other, those students are equally likely to be below the cutoff in the spring, and indeed they may be joined by some students whose true scores are slightly above the cutoff but who were penalized by chance factors in the second administration. The general principle, then, is that any time we select a group of students because they are extreme on a single measurement they will be extreme partly because they are extreme, but partly also because chance happened to fall in the direction that makes them extreme on this one occasion.

One of the consequences of this effect is that there will be a negative relationship between this measure of raw gain or raw change and the pretest. That is, low-scoring pupils tend to move up relative to other pupils and high-scoring pupils tend to lose ground relative to other pupils, and this produces a negative correlation. Out of curiosity, we have run correlations for raw gains of groups of third- through sixth-grade pupils on several subtests of the *Iowa Tests of Basic Skills* (Hieronymus and Linquist, 1971) and found that they range from −.30 to −.50. When one-third length tests for first-grade disadvantaged students were used in a national evaluation study, the correlations ranged from −.60 to −.90. Gain scores are generally less related to pretest scores than are measures of pupil status at the end of the year, but they are still related to such a degree that the mean gain in the individual teacher's classroom is quite likely to be substantially affected by the pretest standing of her pupils.

The regression effect is likely to have important consequences for teachers and principals who are not aware of it. The principal who looks at score changes of pupils throughout his school may expect to find that pupils who make high pretest scores somehow do not seem to do very well. The principal is likely to reach the conclusion that the school program is very satisfactory for low-ability pupils, but seems to have a strangely stultifying effect on bright pupils. If the students are grouped and assigned to individual teachers on the basis of test scores, more serious consequences may occur. Let us assume that a reading test is administered to all the third graders in the school and then the low-scoring readers are assigned to Miss Smith, the middle group to Miss Jones, and the high-scoring group to Miss Williams. When the students are all tested again at the end of the year the results are, unfortunately, highly predictable. Miss Smith, who was assigned the low group, is likely to show a very satisfactory overall gain in her class, whatever she does. Miss Williams, on the other hand, is likely to be in trouble regardless of the effort and skill she may put into teaching her initially high-scoring group. Miss Jones is the only one who might receive a fair evaluation.

One of the authors was an unsuspecting beneficiary of this phenomenon. Early in his teaching career he was asked to teach remedial reading to the 25 junior high school pupils who had the lowest reading test scores in a group of 150. After three months of instruction, the 25 pupils were retested and showed a mean gain of four years in reading ability! The fact that they would have shown almost as spectacular an improvement without a single day of instruction was not suspected by the teacher, his supervisor, or the parents.

It is important to emphasize that *all* of the commonly used methods of estimating mean gains in achievement as measures of teacher effectiveness are susceptible to this effect, and that they can not yield unbiased estimates of teacher effectiveness unless the pupils have been randomly assigned to teachers' classes (cf. Campbell and Erlebacher, 1971). In Appendix C we present an alternative method of estimating teacher effectiveness which seems to be free from this bias, but is still susceptible to errors due to the limited validities and reliabilities of achievement tests.

Limitations of Achievement Tests

Our final problem with pupil gain measures as a basis for evaluating teachers would remain even if they were valid and reliable in the sense in which we have used the terms. This is the likelihood that, because of the limits to what available achievement tests can measure, their use could still have a strong negative effect on the average quality of teaching in any system that uses them to evaluate teachers.

In schools where teachers are evaluated on the basis of how well their pupils do on achievement tests, it is to be expected that teachers will soon adopt raising pupils' test scores as their major if not their only objective. It is to be expected, also, that teachers who can not or will not do so will tend to be eliminated as the tests inevitably come to determine what kind of learning takes place in those schools.

The goals of education are typically defined in rather extravagant terms. Such laudable aims as helping pupils learn to live with themselves and each other, to become valuable members of society, to become critical consumers and life-long learners, etc., are bandied about. Our better teachers take these goals seriously and try to help pupils move toward them. But progress toward such goals is difficult to achieve, and even more difficult to measure, especially over a short period of time.

The standardized tests schools use to measure pupil achievement tend to be highly reliable and reasonably easy and inexpensive to administer and score. They tend to measure pupil progress toward important but less elevated goals of education, because such things as computational skill, knowledge of principles and facts, and the ability to recognize points made in brief prose passages adapt themselves readily to measurement with paper-and-pencil tests.

There is evidence in the research literature which indicates that the kind of teaching that maximizes progress toward the simpler objectives—the ones measured by such tests—differs from the kind of teaching that maximizes progress toward the more complex ones—the ones not measured by such tests (Soar and Soar, 1983).

It should be obvious that if teacher evaluation is based on the gains on standardized achievement tests made by a teacher's pupils, if a teacher's future in the profession depends on how well she achieves these simpler goals, then there will be an increase in the kind of teaching that produces low-level gains and a steady decrease in the kind of teaching that produces high-level gains.

This tendency can only increase if instead of standardized tests the evaluations depend on pupils' scores on the criterion-referenced tests that have recently become so popular, since these tests are designed to measure only the most rudimentary and elementary kinds of pupil achievement.

Another effect to be expected is what happened a century ago when some English schools adopted this scheme of basing teacher evaluations upon gains of pupils (Small, 1972). The teachers in these schools soon realized that there were three kinds of pupils in their classes: some who were likely to pass the tests without any help from the teacher; some who were unlikely to pass them no matter what the teacher did, and some who could pass them only with the teacher's help. Before long, most of the teachers were spending most of their time with the third group, neglecting both the slowest and the brightest pupils in their classes. These were the teachers who were identified as the best by the evaluation system. Clearly, this kind of evaluation did not improve the quality of teaching in those schools.

We may summarize our discussion of the use of pupil's achievement test scores for teacher evaluation by saying that both the validity and the reliability of such evaluation procedures are far too low to be useful. The basic difficulty arises from the multiplicity of factors not under the teacher's control that affect pupil achievement, the operation of which prevents the most competent teachers from obtaining the highest scores and the least competent from obtaining the lowest scores. An additional difficulty arrises from the fact that available achievement tests do not measure some of the most important outcomes of teaching. The consequence is that the poorer teachers often do as well or better than the better teachers.

Additionally, we raise the question of whether a group of students might organize themselves to do poorly on a year-end exam, simply to punish a teacher. We find this easy to imagine, especially in the case of a teacher who expects work from students who have little interest in school achievement. If this could happen, then a system of teacher evaluation based on student achievement puts a club in the students' hands.

Finally, although these difficulties are not insuperable, they can be overcome only by means too costly to justify the effect. And if they were overcome, such evaluations would be severely limited in their usefulness because they would neither be timely nor diagnostic. If they did identify teachers in need of remedial training, it would take them a year to do so, and they would provide no clue as to what kind of remediation was needed.

INFERRING TEACHER COMPETENCE
FROM RATINGS OF PERFORMANCE

In the preceding pages we have given some of the reasons why neither paper-and-pencil tests administered to teachers nor achievement tests administered to their pupils provide the kind of evaluations of teachers that are needed as a basis for improving the quality of instruction in the schools. Neither the quality of teaching in a classroom nor the competence of the teacher who provides it can be predicted from existing teacher competency tests or inferred from outcomes the teacher produces measured by achievement tests presently available.

Can the quality of teaching be measured directly? Can the ability of the teacher to demonstrate competent teaching, that is, the teacher's competence, be inferred from samples of her performance in the classroom? Efforts to do this in the past have been based on the use of teacher rating scales. The teacher rating scale came into general use almost three quarters of a century ago, when one of the yearbooks of the *National Society for the Study of Education* was devoted to the description of a teacher rating scale and a report of empirical studies of its usefulness (Boyce, 1915). Readers who have access to a copy should read this pioneer study, if for no other reason than to note how little the instrument described differs from those in present use, and to ponder how many of the few changes made may be regarded as improvements. The device seems to have met a very real need; by 1930, it was possible to collect no fewer than 209 rating forms then in use (Barr and Emans, 1930).

There are three problems with rating scales as devices for assessing teacher performance which we propose to discuss. One is the fact that they lack the minimum properties necessary for performance measurement; the second is that they lack validity; and the third is that they are highly susceptible to the halo effect.

The Rating Scale as a Measurement Device

We have listed in the preceding chapter the four essential steps or phases in the process of performance evaluation; the first three of these define the process of measurement upon which the evaluation is based. The rating scale does not qualify as a device for measuring teacher performance, mainly because it does not yield a record of the performance, and as a result, cannot be scored objectively. The number which is recorded by the rater is not a score derived by applying a scoring key to a record but a number subjectively abstracted or inferred from the behavior.

Suppose, for instance, that a rater rates a teacher's instructional skill at point two on a scale from one to five. The number two reflects an inference made by the rater about the teacher's instructional skill supposedly based on the teacher's behavior; but there is no record of what the teacher did or did not do which led the rater to rate her skill at level two. Nor is there any indication of how the teacher's behavior would need to change so that she could get a higher rating next time. Ratings are sometimes referred to as *high inference measures*; this phrase is accurate in implying that a high level of inference is required of the rater; but it is inaccurate in calling ratings measures, which they are not.

A structured observation schedule, on the other hand, is sometimes called a *low inference measure*, with considerable accuracy. Each item on such a schedule defines a specific behavior (or category of behaviors) that the recorder looks for and records when he sees it. The record he makes is a record of behaviors; the judgments or high inferences that lead to a score are made beforehand and incorporated into a scoring key which is applied to the record after it is complete. Figure 3.2 compares the two processes. Note that the observer using a structured observation schedule responds only to the behaviors specified by the system, and that his only task is to recognize ("!") these behaviors and record them. Note that the rater may respond to these same behaviors, to other behaviors relevant to the instructional skill of the teacher, or to any other behaviors he sees. His task is to infer or judge ("?") what rating the teacher should get from whatever he sees.

The record made on the observation schedule is processed through a computer (or by a clerk) to yield a score. This process is reversible: it is possible to trace any score back to the behaviors on which it is based. This is not possible with a rating. To paraphrase the poet Browning: "When the rating was made only God and the rater knew what it meant, now only God knows."

To illustrate the problem further, imagine three raters supposed to rate a teacher's overall competence. One rater sees the maintenance of order as a major element in teacher competence and looks for evidence of it when he rates a teacher. A second rater believes that creating a climate which favors responsible pupil independence is essential and looks for that. A third feels that only the way in which the teacher presents her subject matter is important.

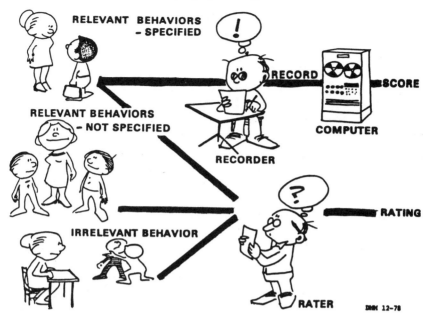

FIGURE 3.2 The recorder and the rater.

All three observe in the same classroom at the same time to rate the teacher's overall competence. During the observation one of the pupils gets up, crosses the room to get a book, and returns to his seat. The first rater perceives this as a violation of classroom order; the second sees it as an example of responsibly independent behavior; the third disregards it as irrelevant. Later in putting together what he has seen in preparation for rating the teacher, the first rater weights the behavior positively, the second weights it negatively and the third gives it no weight at all. Finally, each rater compares his composite picture of the classroom with his own standard and records a rating of the teacher's general competence.

Three observers using an observation schedule which included this item would all record that it had occurred without regard to its relevance, and the three records would all be scored on the same key so that the teacher's score would be the same no matter who the observer was.

What was recorded on the rating scale would depend on: (1) what each rater thought the teacher ought to have been doing; (2) what behaviors he took into account; (3) the weight he attached to each behavior he observed; and (4) the reference standard with which he compared what he saw in arriving at his rating. None of these is known to anyone else. Since all four of these factors vary from one observer to another, so will the ratings the teacher gets.

One thing that may occur to you as you read this is how much simpler it must be to construct a rating scale than it is to develop a scoring key for a true measuring instrument. This simplicity is achieved by leaving all of the critical and difficult decisions to the rater, by leaving it to him to decide which teacher behaviors are relevant and what weights to attach to each, in addition to observing and remembering the behaviors he sees. He must do this in the field either during his visit to the teacher or within a few minutes after it ends. If decisions about relevance and weighting are difficult for you to make wisely when you are developing a scoring key and have ample time to deliberate and consult the literature and your colleagues, how can you expect your rater to make them wisely under the conditions in which he works? It is our contention that the task of recording behavior accurately and objectively is about all an observer can handle successfully.

As you will learn when you read Chapter 8 of this volume, each scoring key for a low-inference instrument combines the frequencies of a number of different behaviors with different weights. Once data on a sizeable sample of classrooms are available it becomes possible to use modern statistical techniques to study the internal structure of a scoring key or set of keys and to revise the scoring weights to improve them. In doing so, important insights are gained into the structure of classroom behavior which are impossible to obtain from ratings. Ratings reflect beliefs of raters about what goes with what, but they do not test the validity of these beliefs. The beliefs upon which a scoring key is based are visible in the weights assigned the individual items of behavior, and a factor analysis of the items on the key provides a most valuable empirical test of those beliefs.

In some of our own research studies we have conducted such analyses and found that some of our own beliefs do not coincide with reality. Most rating scales, for example, reflect a belief that affective classroom climate is a bipolar dimension with negative affect (hostility and mistrust) at one extreme and positive affect (praise and warmth) at the other. But analyses of objective records of behavior reveal that expressions of negative and positive affect are relatively independent. There are some teachers who express both positive and negative affect freely—there is no question how they feel at any moment. There are other teachers who express only positive affect, and still others who express primarily negative affect. Finally, there are some teachers who express little affect of any kind. Such teachers often run task-focused, smooth-running classrooms in which most activities are routine and affect seems irrelevant.

How would the first kind of teacher be rated on a bipolar scale of affective climate? The rater would see her express a great deal of both positive and negative affect, of behavior at both ends of the scale. Most probably he would put her in the middle of the scale to represent his perception that positive and negative affect are approximately evenly balanced. But how would he rate the teacher who expresses little or no affect of either kind? Such a teacher would also fall in the middle of the scale to indicate that neither extreme occurred in her classroom. These are quite different teachers. The fact that both would get the same rating illustrates the inadequacy of a rating scale based on incorrect beliefs about the structure of teacher behavior (Soar and Soar, 1980).

A somewhat more subtle example arises when teachers are rated on the degree to which they ask broad questions. There is some evidence that two dimensions are involved here, too. Teachers may ask questions which expect pupils to go beyond the information given—broad questions—with or without expecting any evaluation of the ideas produced. Idea production may be the end in view, as in a brainstorming session. Or teachers may ask questions which encourage pupils to examine their own ideas to see how well they fit reality. The objective here relates to critical thinking, perhaps, and the pupils' answers are evaluated. A rating scale which asks for the frequency with which a teacher asks broad questions would not recognize this difference (which is manifest in the way the teacher responds) and again, very different performances would get similar ratings (Soar and Soar, 1980).

We have also found clear evidence that teacher control of behavior, of the nonsubstantive activities of pupils, should be distinguished from teacher control of learning activities, because the two types of controlling behaviors relate differently to learning outcomes (Soar and Soar, 1979).

We cite these examples as strongly indicating a need for this kind of structural analysis of teacher performance measurements as a basis for testing the assumptions about teacher behavior which underlie any teacher evaluation device, and changing those assumptions if they do not fit the realities of the classroom. Unless and until we do this we cannot hope to develop valid evaluation procedures.

The fact that rating scales cannot readily be improved in this way is a serious limit to their value. The validity of rating scales depends almost entirely on the accuracy of the beliefs or assumptions about the nature of competent teacher performance upon which they are based. If the beliefs are accurate, the rating scales may be valid. If the beliefs are inaccurate the rating scales cannot possibly yield valid evaluations, and we have a serious problem, because such ratings are the basis of the vast majority of decisions about teachers made by teacher educators, school administrators, and (in recent years) by those responsible for certifying teachers. If all of these decisions are based on evaluations that lack validity, one would expect that there would be serious consequences for education. An incompetent teacher might be expected to have as good a chance as, or a better chance than, a competent teacher of being certified, hired, given tenure, and even receiving merit pay. There are many critics of education who maintain that this is exactly what is happening, and some of them point to evidence that they are right.

It is curious to note that despite these signs that all is not well, the validity of rating scales is rarely questioned, and even more rarely tested empirically. The validity of rating scales is defended by demonstrating that the scales faithfully reflect a consensus of the beliefs or assumptions most educators hold about the nature of competent teacher performance; and there is little reason to doubt that the ratings do reflect those beliefs.

But what about the beliefs? Do they correspond with reality? If the beliefs we all hold are even partially false, the validity of the ratings is open to question. Whether pupils learn more from teachers with high ratings than from teachers with low ratings; or even whether teachers with high ratings exhibit more behaviors known to relate positively to pupil learning than teachers with low ratings—these are empirical questions which no one seems to ask. The only thing we can say with confidence is that high-rated teachers make better impressions on us than low-rated teachers. Is that enough? We think not.

This problem first began to worry us about 25 years ago when we included administrators' and supervisors' ratings (of teachers' effectiveness in fostering subject matter learning) in a study whose major focus was on the relationships between scores on low-inference measures and pupil outcomes (Medley and Mitzel, 1958). We found no relationship whatsoever between the ratings and pupil learning (Medley and Mitzel, 1959). (The ratings did, however, relate to low-inference measures of emotional climate in the classroom and to pupil perceptions of teacher-pupil rapport, neither of which was correlated with pupil learning either.) When we reviewed the literature we found a few other studies in each of which the relationship between ratings and measured pupil achievement gains had also been estimated. Each study reported the same result; no relationship. Each study reached the same conclusion independently: that ratings made by reasonably sophisticated observers of classroom performance had no validity as predictors of teacher effectiveness.

This raised a serious problem for teacher effectiveness researchers as well as for educational decision makers, since ratings of teacher effectiveness made by administrators or supervisors were often used by researchers as the criterion of effective teaching. It also raised questions about the beliefs about effective teaching that were prevalent in the profession, and in turn about the content of teacher education programs. Could some of what we trained teachers to do be making them *less* effective instead of more effective?

The republication of these findings (Medley and Mitzel, 1963) did not have any visible impact on teacher evaluators or teacher educators (who perhaps do not read the research literature); but the researchers (who apparently do) soon abandoned the use of ratings as criteria of teacher effectiveness.

Until recently, no one has bothered to replicate this research; no one has asked whether modern beliefs about teacher effectiveness are any more dependable than those held 20 years or more ago. As part of a study designed to develop a low-inference teacher certification instrument, (Coker et al., 1980) educators' beliefs were tested in a different way. A group of teachers was asked to study current lists of competencies created by teacher educators to define objectives of teacher education programs, and to select from them a set of generic competencies that they regarded as necessary for success as a teacher in their school system. Next, a number of well developed and tested observation instruments which contained low-inference items that appeared to reflect the presence of these competencies were identified. Pupils in a sample of 100 classrooms were tested at the beginning and end of the same school year on measures of attitudes and achievement, and behaviors in each classroom were observed in the interim and recorded on the selected low-inference observation instruments. Researchers who were knowledgeable about each of the observation instruments developed scoring keys which appeared to measure behavioral indicators of the competencies. Scores on these indicators were correlated with measures of pupil gains, both cognitive and affective. Most of the several thousand correlations calculated were not large enough to be statistically significant. Of those that were, about half were negative and half positive.

Apparently what these teachers (and the experts who made the original lists) regarded as behaviors that indicate effective teaching were about as likely to indicate ineffective teaching instead (Coker et al., 1980). In a subsequent, more sophisticated analysis of some of the same data the behavioral indicators were correlated separately with achievement gains of pupils of high and low ability. When this was done 25 percent of the correlations calculated were found to be statistically significant (Lara, 1983), and the same split in signs was found. Half of the correlations, significant and nonsignificant alike, were negative. Behaviors believed to indicate effective teaching were just as likely to indicate ineffective teaching.

It is also worth mentioning that process-product research using low-inference measures has produced some relatively consistent findings, about as many of which contradict commonly held beliefs as confirm them (Medley, 1977). One of the most surprising of these studies was a meta-analysis which found that expressions of positive affect in the classroom (to which teacher educators appear to be committed) have an overall relationship with student achievement of only .07 (Wilkinson, 1980).

A final example which also strikes at a central practitioner belief is some evidence that neither the size of the groups in which teachers organize pupils for instruction nor the degree to which the teacher individualizes instruction may be related to achievement outcome. The evidence suggests that individual or small-group instruction or individualization of instruction is associated with less learning rather than more (Medley, 1979). A meta-analysis of experimental tests of individualized secondary mathematics instruction found significantly greater learning for the control condition (Johnson, 1979). These results suggest that in order for ratings to be valid, raters will have to give high ratings to teachers who behave in ways which the raters themselves do not believe to be effective. Whether this is possible is related to the next problem we propose to discuss, the problem of *halo*.

Halo

A question raised long ago about ratings of any kind is whether a rater might not in effect use each of the different scales on a rating instrument as another opportunity to express his overall impression of how competent the person being rated is. This would result in high positive correlations between ratings of presumably independent characteristics, an effect known as halo.

Cooper (1981) has summarized data on the halo effect, and makes it clear that it is a problem of current concern. He says:

> Plausible but invalid theories can help us see correlations between categories when there is no correlation. . .if we have minimal reasons to believe categories covary, we are prone to rate as if they did covary in specific cases; uncertain, judgmental settings are situations in which such theories are most likely to be used. (p. 225)

Some findings of Dickson and Wiersma (1980) are relevant. These researchers factor analyzed ratings of a group of student teachers on the TPAI, the rating scale currently being used to certify teachers in the state of Georgia (Capie et al., 1979). They found that a single factor accounted for most of the variance in the 19 competencies rated. This factor accounted for about eight times as much variance as any other factor; it loaded on such a variety of characterizations of the teacher that it is difficult to see any common thread. The interpretation which seems most parsimonious is that this factor measures halo—the overall impression that the teacher makes on the rater. A more recent study confirmed this finding (Dickson et al., 1982).

In conclusion, we question the validity of teacher rating scales and of evaluations based on them, mainly on the grounds that at best they reflect the beliefs of the rater about the nature of competent teacher performance rather than the actual competence of the performance, and that the two may be quite different. What empirical data there are indicate that teachers rated high are no more effective on the average in producing pupil achievement gains than teachers rated low on such instruments.

The nature of ratings makes it difficult if not impossible to discover why any one of a set of ratings may be invalid, both because the halo effect operates to obscure what is actually being rated, and because the behavioral basis of any rating cannot be ascertained by any kind of analysis of data based on the ratings themselves. Ratings are therefore useless for diagnosis and can add nothing to our understanding of the teaching process.

SUMMARY

We have examined the experience of the profession with the three main strategies of teacher evaluation that have been used in the past and have found them all wanting as ways of measuring teacher competence. Results of paper-and-pencil tests administered to teachers have so far failed to predict how well they perform. Measures of teacher effectiveness based on test scores of pupils are neither reliable nor valid enough to tell us anything about how competent a teacher is. Most of the differences in pupil performance are attributable to influences other than the teacher. And ratings of teacher performance tell us only how favorable an impression a teacher makes on the rater, a piece of information that has little or no connection with how competent the teacher is.

We have also noted that the use of any one of these strategies is worse than useless because it may be harmful. Paper-and-pencil tests administered at inappropriate points in the teacher's career can result in real injustices to the teacher. The use of measures of average gains of pupils in teachers' classes for evaluating individual teachers are as likely to reduce the quality of teaching in a system as to increase it. And rating scales reflect a set of beliefs which often leads teacher educators to train teachers in ways that decrease their effectiveness instead of increasing it.

That there is a need for a better way of evaluating teachers seems clear. Indeed, the need is urgent. What we shall describe in the pages to follow is an alternative approach which has been designed to be free of the faults of the approaches described in this chapter. Whether it will work or not is an empirical question. But the evidence to date suggests that it is more likely to succeed than any of the procedures now in common use.

BIBLIOGRAPHY

Anderson, G. J. "Effects of Classroom Climate on Individual Learning." *American Educational Research Journal*, 1970, 7, 135–152.

Barr, A. S. "Measurement and Prediction of Teacher Efficiency." *Journal of Experimental Education*, 1948, 16, 203–283.

Barr, A. S., and L. M. Emans. "What Qualities are Prerequisite to Success in Teaching?" *National Schools*, 1930, 6, 60–64.

Boyce, A. C. "Methods of Measuring Teachers' Efficiency." *Fourteenth Yearbook of the National Society for Study of Education, Part II*. Bloomington, IL: Public School Publishing Co., 1915.

Brophy, J. E. "Stability in Teacher Effectiveness." *American Educational Research Journal*, 1970, 10, 245–252.

Campbell, D. T., and A. Erlebacher. "How Regression Artifacts in Quasi-Experimental Evaluations Can Mistakenly Make Compensatory Education Look Harmful." In J. Hellmuth, ed., *The Disadvantaged Child*. vol. 3, New York, Brunner/Mazel, 1971.

Capie, W. et al. *Teacher Performance Assessment Instruments*. Athens, GA: University of Georgia, School of Education, 1979, ED182518.

Coker, Homer, Donald Medley, and Robert Soar. "How Valid are Expert Opinions about Effective Teaching?" *Phi Delta Kappan*, 1980, 62 (2), 131–134; 149.

Coleman, J. S. *The Adolescent Society*. New York: Free Press, 1961.

Cooper, W. H. "Ubiquitous Halo." *Psychological Bulletin*, 1981, 90, 218–244.

D'Amico, S. D. "The Relationship of Clique Membership to Achievement, Self-Concept, Social Acceptance and School Attitude." Ph. D. diss., University of Florida, 1973.

Dickson, G. E., S. G. Jurs, J. Wenig, and W. Wiersma. "The Analysis and Interpretation of Student Teacher Observation Data Used for Measuring Teacher Competencies." Paper read at American Educational Research Association meeting, New York, March, 1982.

Dickson, G. E., and W. Wiersma. *Research and Evaluation in Teacher Education: A Concern for Competent, Effective Teachers*. Toledo, OH: The University of Toledo, May, 1980.

Gage, N. L., ed. *Handbook of Research on Teaching*. Chicago: Rand McNally, 1963.

Garber, M., and W. B. Ware. "The Home Environment as A Predictor of School Achievement." *Theory Into Practice*, Columbus, OH: Ohio State Univesity Press, 1972, 11, 190–195.

Hieronymus, A. N., and E. F. Lindquist. *Iowa Tests of Basic Skills*. Boston: Hougton Mifflin, 1971.

Lara, A. V. "Pupil Ability as a Moderator of Correlations between Teacher

Behavior Patterns and Pupil Gains in Reading and Mathematics." Ph. D. diss., University of Virginia, Charlottesville, 1983.

Johnson, P. I. "The Relationship of Self-Paced Individualized Instruction to Pupil Achievement When Measured by Pooling the Probabilities of Several Independent Samples." Ph.D. diss., University of Florida, 1979.

Medley, Donald M. *Teacher Competence and Teacher Effectiveness, A Review of Process-Product Research.* Washington, DC: American Association of Colleges for Teacher Education, 1977.

——— "The Effectiveness of Teachers," In Penelope L. Peterson and Herbert J. Walberg, eds., *Research on Teaching.* Berkeley, CA: McCutchan, 1979.

Medley, Donald M., and Harold E. Mitzel. "A Technique for Measuring Classroom Behavior." *Journal of Educational Psychology*, 1958, 49, 86–92.

——— "Some Behavioral Correlates of Teacher Effectiveness." *Journal of Educational Psychology*, 1959, 50, 239–246.

——— "Measuring Classroom Behavior by Systematic Observation." In N. L. Gage, ed., *Handbook of Research on Teaching*, Chicago, IL: Rand McNally, 1963.

North Carolina Department of Education. "Facts behind the Figures: School Effectiveness Study." Mustafa E. Konanc, Donald Ferguson, and Evan Sun, eds. Raliegh, NC: Author, 1980.

Quirk, T. J., B. J. Witten, and S. F. Weinberg. "Review of Studies of the Concurrent and Predictive Validity of the National Teacher Examinations." *Review of Educational Research*, 1973, 43, 89–113.

Rosenshine, B. "The Stability of Teacher Effects upon Student Achievement." *Review of Educational Research*, 1970, 40, 647–662.

Small, A. A. "Accountability in Victorian England." *Phi Delta Kappan*, 1972, 53, 438–439.

Soar, Robert S., and Ruth M. Soar. "Classroom Behavior, Pupil Characteristics and Pupil Growth for the School Year and the Summer." *JSAS Catalog of Selected Documents in Psychology*, 1975, 5 (200), (ms. no. 873).

——— "Emotional Climate and Management." In R. E. Peterson and H. J. Walberg, eds. *Research on Teaching.* Berkeley, CA: McCutchan, 1979.

——— "Setting Variables, Classroom Interaction and Multiple Pupil Outcomes." *JSAS Catalog of Selected Documents in Psychology*, 1980, 10, ms. no. 2110.

——— "Context Effects in the Teaching-Learning Process." In *Essential Knowledge for Beginning Educators*, David C. Smith, ed. Washington, DC: AACTE and Eric Clearinghouse, in press.

Travers, Robert M., ed. *Second Handbook of Research on Teaching.* Chicago: Rand-McNally, 1973.

Wilkinson, S. S. "The Relationship of Teacher Praise and Student Achievement: A Meta-Analysis of Selected Research." Ph. D. diss., University of Florida, 1980.

Part II

Procedures for Measuring Teacher Performance

4

Defining the Dimensions of Performance to Be Evaluated

The most difficult task that will face you if you decide to abandon the rating scale and adopt a measurement-based approach to teacher evaluation is probably the first. Your first task will be to define specifically and in detail just what you mean by each dimension of teacher performance you propose to measure. This will almost certainly be something you have never done before. You should begin by identifying a set of dimensions along which you believe the performances of competent teachers differ from those of incompetent ones. You may come up with terms like *instructional skill, ability to control a class, individualizing instruction, concern for pupils' self-images,* or *maintaining an orderly but emotionally supportive environment.*

If you were planning to evaluate teacher performance by rating it, your next task would be to look for a teacher rating instrument that contained a scale for rating each dimension from one to five (or maybe from one to ten). You would select an instrument which purported to measure most or all the dimensions you consider important, and you would do so mainly on the basis of the *name* attached to each rating scale.

This is a deceptively simple task because you can do it without having to face up to the really difficult task of defining exactly what you mean, for example, by an *orderly but emotionally supportive environment,* or the even more difficult task of getting some team or committee to agree on a definition. All you do is name the dimension and then leave it to

55

the observer who makes the rating to figure out what that name means.

If you plan to use a structured observation system to measure performance instead of rating it, you cannot avoid this disagreeable task because you must provide the observer with a schedule or list of specific behaviors that he will be looking for and recording. Your observer need not, and preferably should not, even know what dimensions you are trying to measure or which of them any specific behavior is relevant to.

The process we are talking about involves three steps: first, *choosing the dimensions* of teacher performance you propose to evaluate; second, defining each dimension provisionally by *specifying behaviors* whose occurrence in the classroom indicate where a teacher stands on each dimension; and third, *looking for a structured observation system* that has already been developed and used successfully which yields records of most or all of the specified behaviors.

In this chapter we will discuss the first and second steps; our discussion of the third will be postponed until we get to Chapter 5.

If we are correct in assuming that you plan to use your evaluations to improve instruction by upgrading the competence of some group of teachers, we strongly advise you to work with the group (or its representatives) from the very beginning, establishing agreement about what the basis of the evaluation is to be among all concerned. Such a consensus will, as we shall see later, greatly facilitate the completion of the first step in the process of performance evaluation—defining the task—by ensuring that every teacher agrees on, or at least understands, what she must do to earn a positive evaluation, and why.

A Hierarchical Organization

One way to simplify the task of reaching such a consensus is to arrange both general and specific descriptions of competent behavior in a hierarchy so that the behaviors specified are seen as parts of more broadly defined dimensions. Figure 4.1 is an incomplete example of what we mean.

The first row across the top of the chart represents the highest level of abstraction in the diagram; it includes relatively broad statements about what a teacher should be or do in order to perform competently. In this instance, the assertion is that growth of the child is facilitated by an orderly but emotionally supportive environment.

Disagreement with this statement is not likely. Perhaps this reflects the fact that at this level of abstraction the statement does not really have enough concrete meaning so that you could either agree or disagree with it. You can get agreement on almost anything if you go high enough up the abstraction ladder; if you become sufficiently abstract, you are using words that mean different things to different people and

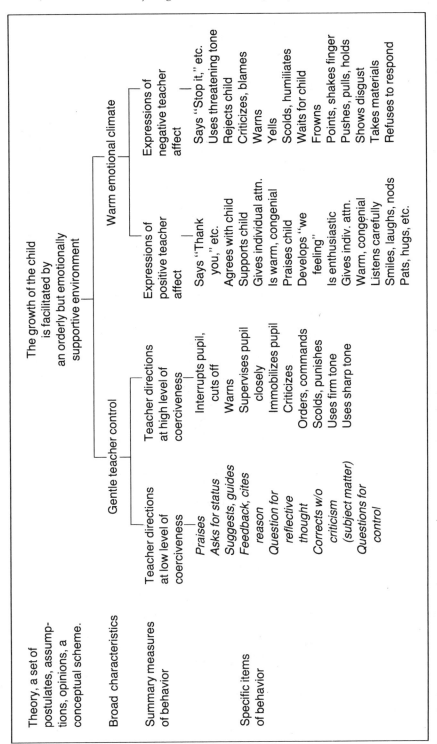

FIGURE 4.1 A behavioral hierarchy. (Those items in italics are defined in the *Climate and Control System: Observer's Manual*, Soar and Soar, 1980.)

everyone is agreeing with his own meaning. Just the same, it is useful, almost necessary, to begin with such a common base.

In the next row of the figure, in which we begin to break the broad statement down, we begin to face differences within the group which must be recognized and dealt with. These differences must be resolved at each level in turn as we become more concrete and specific.

Returning to the example, we have listed two clear aspects of the initial statement at the next level on which we will assume agreement has been reached. One is that the order must be obtained by gentle or noncoercive means if the environment is to remain supportive. The other is that there must be a warm emotional climate. These two statements are listed on the second level of the hierarchy, called *broad characteristics*. Although more concrete than the statement above them, these behaviors are still not objectively measureable. Observers will still differ, for instance, on how warm is *warm*. These behaviors are recognized to be characteristics of desirable classroom behavior, but they are still not specified in enough detail to be objectively assessable.

At the third level, we begin to identify what may be called *summary measures of behavior* that are recognized as components or aspects of the broader characteristics. Each summary measure is made up in turn of *specific items of behavior* which can be defined with the care necessary for inclusion in a manual of instruction for classroom observers. Items must eventually be specified in enough detail so that an observer can be trained to recognize reliably each item of behavior that he sees occur during a period of observation, and so that the teacher herself can tell whether she has exhibited any one of them. This fourth level of the hierarchy, the most specific, provides the basis for obtaining a scorable record of behavior.

As an example at this most specific level, the item *suggests, guides* might refer to such teacher statements as, "How about putting it over there, Jimmy, OK?" "I wonder if you would shut the door for us, Bill?" and "Bob, would you mind moving so John can sit down?" These statements are suggestions for change in behavior that have the characteristic of being softened by a "please" or "OK"?, or by being phrased as questions (Soar, Soar, and Ragosta 1971).

Another item at the gentlest level of control, *feedback, cites reason,* is coded when the teacher gives information which implies a change in behavior without directly asking for it. For example, the teacher comment "I'm having trouble hearing" is not a direction, but it does give information which implies a change in behavior without directly asking for it. We observed an instance in a first-grade classroom during the first week of class. The number one and number two trouble makers (two boys who could be so identified in five minutes) were together in the back row of a small group, jostling, nudging, and pinching. The teacher looked at one of them and said, "John, I think there's room for you up here," gestured toward a spot by her feet, and waited. In two or three seconds, John came to sit by the teacher's feet. The other pupils did not seem to see it as a put-down; but it did create a big gap between the two trouble makers and the problem was solved.

At an intermediate level of coerciveness (not shown in the figure) would be statements such as, "OK, anyone who wants to go to the bathroom, get in line," which is not very coercive, but clearly a direction with a reason. Other examples would be: "Get out your arithmetic books and open them to page 27." "When you've finished, put your papers on my desk."

At the coercive end of the scale would be a statement like, "Jimmy, stop that!" which would be coded *orders, commands*, and probably *sharp tone* as well.

Using a hierarchy like the one described above lets us talk about particular aspects of a rather vague concept like "orderly but emotionally supportive environment" in terms of a series of relatively objective statements about teacher behavior. If each specific behavior is defined with sufficient care so that agreement between observers can be made acceptably high, we can reliably assess this aspect of behavior.

The lists of specific behaviors should be as long as possible because chances are that no existing instrument will yield a record of all of them, and you will have to settle for one that contains most of them.

Controversial items—ones you cannot get everyone to agree on—should be included at this point. Later on, when you analyze the results you obtain with your instrument, if most of your items are relevant, those that are not will be easily identified by statistical analysis and can be eliminated from the scoring key. Everyone's ideas about the nature of a dimension should be represented, just in case.

Choosing the Dimensions

How do you decide what dimensions to evaluate? On what basis do you decide that an orderly but emotionally supportive environment is important enough to effective teaching to be worth evaluating and making an objective of a program of staff development?

Perhaps you have no problem; maybe you feel that you already know what dimensions of teacher performance are most important or which ones your staff needs to develop the most. If so, what we are proposing is a means for putting your convictions into action.

Those of you who are not quite so sure have at least three different strategies you can use to choose dimensions to evaluate. One is to begin with a plausible *theory* of teaching and to derive specifications of behavior from it. There are a number of such theories in the literature, none of which can be said to have been empirically established, but most of which are worth trying, if you like them (cf. for example, Joyce and Weil, 1980; McDonald and Leeper, 1965; Stiles, 1974).

A second strategy is to use whatever most educators agree constitutes effective teaching. Those who train teachers, those who supervise teachers, will have ideas. Why not survey their *opinions* and develop a system for measuring the dimensions they agree are important?

A third strategy is to turn to the process-product *research*, and select a proven instrument or instruments, used in several studies, which have yielded significant findings. Another alternative is to build an instrument to measure those dimensions of teacher behavior that the research has shown to be related to effectiveness.

It might be wise not to limit yourself to any one approach but to combine two or more. However, in the next few pages we will discuss the processes you might follow in implementing each of them separately. As you will see, each has its strengths and its weaknesses. Which process you follow does not make much difference since any one of them can lead you to the comprehensive set of relevant behaviors which is all you need at the start. If enough relevant behaviors are in your records, deriving valid measurements from them is a relatively straightforward empirical process.

THEORY AS A BASIS FOR DEFINING EFFECTIVE TEACHER PERFORMANCE

The first strategy that we shall discuss for defining the dimensions of teacher performance to be evaluated is to proceed from a theory or model of effective teaching. Instead of discussing the process in abstract or general terms we shall give an example using our own theory (with the understanding that you may adopt the procedure without necessarily adopting the theory).

Our theory has been called a "circus" theory because it visualizes the teacher as operating on three levels or in three "rings" simultaneously: environmental maintenance, implementation of instruction, and individualization.

We assume that, during what Jackson (1966) has identified as the *preactive* phase of teaching, the teacher will have developed an appropriate lesson plan or strategy and a set of objectives for the lesson which she intends to implement during what Jackson calls the *interactive* phase of teaching. The ability to design appropriate instructional plans is an important element in effective teaching, but our concern here is not with the plan but with the teacher's behavior in the classroom as she attempts to implement it, and our evaluation of the teacher will be based on observations of classroom behavior as she does so.

The first thing a teacher must accomplish before she can implement any plan is to create and maintain a classroom environment favorable to learning, and more importantly, to long-term, lifetime learning. Observable teacher behaviors designed to create and maintain such an environment form one basis on which teacher performance will be assessed. So long as the teacher maintains an environment favorable to learning, pupils in her class will learn something; and some of what they learn will result in progress toward the specific objectives the teacher has defined and some will not. It is worth noting that if we could help teachers improve their skills in this area alone we could probably produce a dramatic improvement in instruction in most schools.

When the classroom environment is favorable to learning, further acceleration of pupil progress toward the specific objectives of the lesson depends on implementation of the lesson plan. If pupils perform the activities and have the experiences defined in an appropriate plan, they may be expected to make more progress toward the specific objectives the teacher has defined than they would without these experiences. Observable behaviors of the teacher designed to implement the plan constitute the second basis for assessing teacher performance.

Even when the plan is being implemented, there may be some pupils who, because of motivational factors, disabilities, or other individual characteristics, do not become involved in the appropriate activities. Behaviors of the teacher designed to adapt the plan to maintain involvement of such pupils provide a third basis for evaluating teacher performance.

Figure 4.2 is a dynamic flowchart of the teaching process according to this model. The rectangles in the figure represent the four elements in action: the diamonds represent three points at which the teacher assesses the situation, gets feedback, and makes decisions about what to do next. Such decisions occur very frequently throughout the period.

If the teacher senses at any moment that the learning environment has deteriorated below a certain level, she takes action to alter the environment (the lower feedback loop). If she decides that it has deteriorated below a second level she may decide to abandon the plan (upper loop). If she decides that the environment is above the first level, the teacher moves to the second decision point and evaluates the progress of the plan. If this needs attention, she either adjusts it (lower loop), or abandons the plan (upper loop). If the teacher decides that the plan is being implemented satisfactorily she checks the involvement of individual pupils (third decision point) and makes whatever adaptations are necessary (lower loop), unless too many pupils need to have the plan modified, in which case she abandons the plan (upper loop).

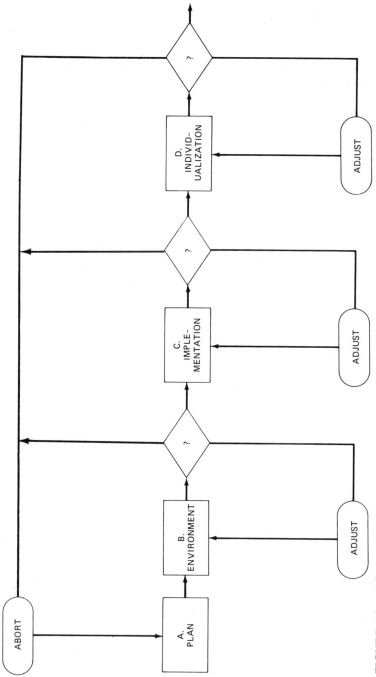

FIGURE 4.2   A flowchart of the dynamics of interactive teaching.

To repeat, although this model has four elements in it, our evaluation will involve only three of them. The first element has to do with preactive teaching and can be measured better in some other way than by observing the teacher's interactive behavior (perhaps by examining her written lesson plans). Our concern here is with the interactive phases only; that is, with *environmental maintenance, implementation of instruction,* and *individualization.*

We must now ask ourselves what kinds of classroom behavior determine how skillful a teacher is in each of these three phases or aspects of interactive teaching; that is, we need to identify a set of summary measures for each of these three aspects.

Learning Environment. The first two broad characteristics of an environment favorable to learning that come to mind are those illustrated in Figure 4.1 and just discussed: gentle teacher control, which provides an orderly environment in which pupils are able to engage in learning experiences with a minimum risk of distraction or disruption, without any of the repressive teacher behaviors that are themselves more disruptive than almost anything else; and a warm emotional climate, which minimizes the fear of failure that inhibits so many pupils. In addition, the environment should be one in which learning itself is valued, is seen as exciting and pleasurable; and perhaps also one in which pupils are constantly challenged to do better today than yesterday.

These and any other broad characteristics you may identify must be further clarified by the identification of summary measures and specific behavior indicators in the manner exemplified in Figure 4.1.

Implementation of Instruction. This aspect of effective teaching is usually seen as made up of such characteristics as skill in presenting lesson content, skill in conducting class group discussions, skill in organizing for instruction and in using instructional aids and materials, and the like. Evaluation of the first of these skills would need to be based on summary measures of skills in explaining, defining, summarizing, etc., each of which calls in turn for the identification of specific items of behavior relevant to that particular skill.

You will not get very far into this process before you find that it is rarely possible to decide whether an item is a positive or negative indicator of skill, that is, whether its occurrence indicates presence or absence of the skill, without specific information about the plan the teacher is trying to implement. Such items as asking a higher-order question, providing negative feedback, or asking a pupil to elaborate on his answer to a question may be positive when one type of plan is being followed and negative when another is being implemented.

Rating scales generally deal with this problem by asking the rater to judge whether the behavior is appropriate or not. You cannot ask your observer to do this: his task is to record whether the behavior occurred; he need not—should not—know or care whether it is appropriate. If you want to measure skill in implementing instruction you will need information about the nature of the plan as well as a behavior record in order to do so. This kind of information is obtained as part of the procedure of defining the task the teacher is performing, which we shall discuss in Chapter 6.

At this stage, then, you should concern yourself only with relevance in considering specific items of behavior; you will need summary measures relevant to all of the types of lesson plans that you expect to see teachers implementing; and you will need items relevant to each of the summary measures you specify.

Individualization of Instruction.   This aspect of teacher performance receives an amount of attention, mainly limited to lip service, far out of proportion to the amount of knowledge that exists about its nature or its contribution to teacher effectiveness. As we shall see, much of what research there is indicates that adapting instruction to individual differences may be so inefficient a use of teacher time as to lessen rather than increase her overall effectiveness.

We have seen that it is not possible to evaluate skill in implementing instruction without using information about the plan being implemented. Similarly, it is not possible to evaluate skill in adapting instruction to individual differences without using information about the individuals involved. And the information needed must be obtained and used in much the same way.

We therefore can and should include in our definition of broad characteristics of teacher performance those that relate to individualization, and should specify summary measures and specific behavior items that are relevant to these characteristics even though we cannot specify whether they are negative or positive indicators without information about the pupils involved.

One such broad characteristic has to do with sensitivity to and the ability to perceive signs of pupils' needs, interest, attitude. Another has to do with skill in eliciting such information from pupils. A third has to do with skill in managing a classroom in which different pupils are engaged in different activities. It should be possible to specify items of behavior relevant to each.

Concluding Remarks.   This rather sketchy example may give you some idea of the process by which a particular theory or model of effective teaching may be dissected to identify items of behavior to be observed in the performance of teachers as a basis for measuring whatever aspects of teacher effectiveness the theory defines.

You may notice that some specific items of behavior come up more than once under different summary measures. This need not concern you too much at this point, but you should consciously seek items of behavior unique to one dimension; if you do not, some of your summary measures are likely to vanish when you analyze your records, and you may have to conclude that your theory has failed to achieve one of its important functions, which is to define facets of teacher performance that can be measured separately and used in diagnosis.

Not that the failure of a theory matters much in itself. One should never take any theoretical model, however plausible, very seriously unless or until it has a strong empirical base. And no existing theory presently has such a base. We will see later how we can use our instrument to test and refine a theory.

How many behavioral indicators should you try to identify before you may feel you have the makings of a viable measurement system? This is difficult to answer. The best we can say is the more the better. You are the best judge of the most important issue, which is whether a set of indicators is sufficiently representative of what you have in mind. If you cannot develop an adequate set, your theory may not yet be well enough developed to be of use.

CONSENSUS AS A BASIS FOR DEFINING EFFECTIVE TEACHER PERFORMANCE

The consensus approach usually involves a survey of the opinions of some defined group about what effective teaching looks like—what effective teachers do that ineffective teachers do not do. In order to be useful for our purposes the survey must be designed to elicit opinions about how effective teachers behave rather than about what personal characteristics they should possess. If possible, the group should include your constituency—the practitioner group in which you propose to use the instrument.

It is certainly logical to go to the experts for guidance in attempts to define dimensions of effective teaching, the experts being the teachers themselves as well as those who train or supervise them. Any profession that lacks an adequate scientific base for defining best practice develops its base by building up a store of common beliefs based on experiences accumulated and passed on for generations.

If the experience of the medical profession is any guide, much of this common set of beliefs is likely to be incorrect (Thomas, 1981). The beliefs are probably accurate in identifying which behaviors are relevant, but they are much less trustworthy indicators of how any specific item of behavior relates to pupil learning—of what weight should be assigned to any particular behavior in your scoring key. Scoring keys based on expert opinion are likely to need much refinement before they yield valid measurements.

Most consensus surveys ask experts to judge the importance of summary measures or perhaps of specific items of behavior (called *competencies*) to success in teaching. This short-circuits the process in Figure 4.1 somewhat. What is important is what behaviors your instrument records, since the validity of your evaluations depends ultimately on these behaviors. A consensus may lead to the right behaviors; if the scoring key is not valid you can change it later.

There are excellent political advantages to using this approach. The instrument you evolve will have face validity; it will *look* valid to the experts and should therefore gain acceptance from your constituency, and keep you in business while you develop scoring keys that are truly valid.

In order to give you a more concrete grasp of the consensual approach in action we will briefly describe an example from our own experience (Medley et al., 1981). In this instance, we decided to develop an evaluation system based on the consensus of the classroom teachers in the single school district in which it was to be used. Three committees made up of teachers from the system were organized; they met regularly to study existing lists of teacher competencies and derive from them a list of summary measures called *behavioral indicators* which we could use to identify successful teachers in their district. The three preliminary lists were reviewed by a schoolwide committee and combined into a single list which identified important areas of competence and also specified one or more behavioral indicators for each area. The final list is shown in Figure 4.3 (pp. 67–69).

With the list in hand, the project staff examined a number of existing observation systems to find out how many behavior items recorded with each system were relevant to one or another of the behavioral indicators on the teachers' list. We found that virtually all of the indicators that pertained to classroom behavior were represented by one or more specific items of behavior recorded on one or another of five existing instruments (Brown, 1970; Medley, 1973; Soar, Soar, and Ragosta, 1971; Spaulding, 1969, 1970), and that more than a few indicators were scorable on two or more instruments.

We therefore decided not to undertake constructing a new instrument, but instead to develop new scoring keys for the existing instruments (for the results, see Medley et al., 1981). As we note in Chapter 5, the decision whether to build a new instrument or use one

Competency Area	Behavioral Indicators	
	Teacher Behaviors	*Pupil Learning Experiences*
1. Organizes pupils, resources & materials for effective instruction	a. Selects goals & objectives appropriate to pupil need b. Matches pupil with appropriate material c. Gathers multilevel materials d. Involves student in organizing & planning	a. Enjoy class, happy smiles, relaxed b. On task, activity involved c. Evidence academic growth d. Absence of withdraw behavior
2. Demonstrates ability to communicate effectively with pupils	a. Gives clear explicit directions which are understood by pupils b. Pauses, elicits and responds to pupil questions before proceeding c. Uses a variety of methods, verbal & nonverbal, to deliver instructions	a. Less confusion, less time wasting b. More relaxed, less frustration c. Self-directed to move toward task
3. Assists pupils in using a variety of relevant communication techniques	a. Demonstrates proper listening skills b. Respects individual's rights to speak c. Utilizes nonverbal communication skills d. Utilizes written language as type of communication	a. Acquire capacity to be good listeners b. Able to speak freely c. Able to follow directions, on task d. Discriminate acceptable from nonacceptable behavior e. Able to communicate through writing
4. Assists pupils in dealing with their misconceptions or confusions, using relevant clues and techniques	a. Utilizes pupil feedback verbal or nonverbal, to modify own teaching behavior b. Demonstrates flexibility in classroom management practices	a. Asks questions b. Feel free to interrupt presentations c. Movement toward tasks

	c. Provides opportunity for pupil-initiated questions d. When pupil not on task, teacher makes contact	
5. Responds appropriately to coping behavior of pupils	a. Maintains self-control in various classroom situations and interactions with pupils b. Recognizes & treats individual pupil behavior c. Seeks appropriate help from others d. Accepts necessity of dealing with individual pupils on individual basis	a. Absence of pupil manipulation b. Modifies behavior positively c. Reduction of disruptive behavior
6. Uses a variety of methods & materials to stimulate & promote pupil learning	a. Uses more than one teaching method in a single presentation b. Adapts methods & materials to instructional situation & established goals & objectives	a. Attending (attentive) behavior b. Motivated c. Actively involved
7. Promotes self-awareness & positive self-concepts in pupils	a. Opportunity for each pupil to meet success daily is provided b. Provides variety of materials dealing with learning levels, interests, values, cultural & socio-economic background c. Evidence of a personal one-to-one relationship with each pupil d. Provides opportunity for pupil to have voice in decision making	a. Working on individual level b. Moving toward self-direction c. Attending to task d. Knowledge of variety of cultural & socioeconomic background e. Evidence of importance as class member—group involvement f. Assume responsibility for own success or failure g. Evidence of enthusiasm

	e. Evidence of praise and/or rewards in operation	
8. Reacts with sensitivity to the needs and feelings of others	a. Accepts & incorporates pupil ideas b. Listens to pupils and provides feedback c. Evidence of an opportunity for one-to-one counseling and absence of evidence that pupils are rejected (brushed off)	a. Express ideas & opinions different to those of the teacher or peers b. High interest c. Pupil-teacher rapport is evident d. Developing sense of belonging e. Evidence of confidence in teacher

FIGURE 4.3 Competencies and behavioral indicators of competence constructed by classroom teachers. (From the *Annual Report* of the Carrol County Competency-Based Teacher Certification Project to the Georgia State Department of Education, Homer Coker, Director, 1974.)

(or more) existing ones is best made when the list of summary measures and, if possible, specific items, is complete.

If you are contemplating using the consensual approach to the development of a set of behavioral indicators, there is a considerable body of relevant literature. Since you may find some of it useful, we will review it briefly here.

For many years research in teacher effectiveness was based on the assumption that how effective a teacher was depended on personal characteristics of the teacher, most of which we will classify today as preexisting teacher characteristics. Such things as *patience, intelligence, affection for children*, and *moral character* were typical. Later on the focus shifted to such traits as *teaching skill, rapport with pupils*, and *acceptance of cultural differences*, which sound more like dimensions of performance to us today.

A considerable literature devoted to listing such traits appeared, culminating in the *Commonwealth Teacher Training Study* (Charters and Waples, 1929). This was an elaborate, carefully designed, and laborious attempt to generate consensus descriptions of effective teachers in terms of adjectives describing traits supposed to distinguish them from ineffective teachers. Such a list is, of course, quite useless for our purpose. A second phase of the study produced an exhaustive list of the activities of teachers. Curiously enough, and unfortunately for our purposes, no attempt was made to study differences in the activities of effective and ineffective teachers.

The Committee on the Criteria of Teacher Effectiveness of the American Educational Research Association in its 1952 report (Barr et al.) emphasized the central role of classroom behavior in teacher effectiveness. Soon after it appeared, Ryans published *Characteristics of Teachers* (1960), a report of a study in which he attempted to implement some of these ideas in a new instrument, the *Classroom Observation Record*. Ryans saw clearly that the important characteristics of teachers are the ones they manifest in their classroom behaviors; unfortunately, his instrument has all the limitations of a rating scale, which is what it is. The *Classroom Observation Record* yielded not an objective record but a set of subjective ratings.

In 1968, in response to a request for proposals from the United States Office of Education, nine teacher education faculties developed nine model programs for training elementary school teachers. In compliance with the request, each model was designed around a detailed list of behavioral objectives. Most of these objectives were teacher competencies, according to our definition of the term, and such programs came to be known as *competency-based teacher education programs*. One by-product of this activity was the *Florida Catalog of Teacher Competencies* (1973), a classified compilation of all the behavioral objectives specified in the nine elementary education models. Strictly speaking, this catalog does not reflect a consensus, but it might be useful as a source of ideas, of competencies to consider.

During the heyday of competency-based teacher education there was a growing interest in competency-based teacher certification and teacher competency testing, which led a number of states to construct lists of competencies which should be required for competency-based certification. In most instances the list was built by obtaining consensus ratings of specific items of behavior from teachers, administrators, and/or teacher educators. Some of these lists may still be available.

If you are interested in basing your teacher evaluation system on such a consensus, you could save considerable time by beginning with one or more of these lists, perhaps eliminating some items and adding a few of your own, and sending the revised list to members of the group whose consensus you wish to obtain, with the request that the items be rated individually as to their (judged) importance. Also of some use may be a somewhat more sophisticated publication which came out of an Office of Education project designed to develop teacher training materials (Smith, 1969), a publication which attempted to catalog all teaching skills important to effective teaching (Turner, n.d.).

When you ask a group to rank order items on a preset list from most to least important, it is essential that your list of specific items of behavior be as complete as possible. If you happened to omit a behavior which everyone thinks is critically important, what you get would not be a true consensus, and whatever validity the procedure may have would be impaired. A typical consensus study, and one which has been particularly influential, is one conducted by the state of Georgia (Johnson et al., 1978).

It seems to us that enough of these studies have already been done to provide all that anyone needs to know about how educators think that effective teachers behave, perhaps more than anyone cares to know. The claims to validity of these lists (and of the rating scales derived from them) rest solely on the fact that their item content reflects what practitioners in their respective state *believe* effective teachers do.

Our own research (Coker, Medley, and Soar, 1980) does not lead us to think that these beliefs are correct, but our opinion does not really matter. A consensus is as good a place to begin as any, but it is not dependable until it has been validated empirically. The differences between lists obtained from different sources tend not to justify the cost and trouble of doing another survey in your jurisdiction, unless political or public relations considerations make such a survey advisable for other reasons. Whether or not your instrument is valid will become apparent after you try it out. If the validity is low, you can increase it at relatively little expense by improving your scoring keys, if you have enough relevant items.

RESEARCH AS A BASIS FOR DEFINING EFFECTIVE TEACHER PERFORMANCE

Although the actual role that research plays in educational decision making is quite small, the idea of basing decisions on research findings has great appeal. Nothing could sound better than to be able to say that your evaluation system is based on only those specific items of behaviors which research has discovered to be correlated with teaching outcomes. But the fact is that only a small part of the domain of effective teacher behavior has been subjected to rigorous research so far, and relatively few significant relationships have been found even in this small domain. If your instrument was limited to those behaviors which research has shown to be significantly related to pupil learning, it would cover only a small part of the range of behaviors that distinguish effective teachers from ineffective ones.

In a review of the research on teacher effectiveness limited to studies that met fairly rigorous standards of quality, we found that virtually all of the well-established findings pertained to teachers whose pupils were classified as disadvantaged and enrolled in the primary grades (Medley, 1977). This is a rather special group of pupils, and the findings cannot, therefore, be expected to apply to pupils in general. These are pupils whose home backgrounds are such that they come to school for the first time less well prepared than other pupils, and the main concern of their teachers is to make up this deficit, especially in reading. The immediate objectives for these children as well as the methods appropriate for achieving them may differ very much from those appropriate with better prepared pupils in the same grade and school, and even more from those appropriate for pupils in the higher grades. Evaluations of teachers in the intermediate or upper grades based on these findings might be invalid, might reward teachers for incompetent performance, and might therefore tend to reduce the effectiveness of instruction in the schools.

Research findings can play a role in your efforts to identify specific items of behavior relevant to effective teaching similar to that of consensus studies. If you make use of tentative, unverified findings you may be able to define a set of research-based behavior items that is comprehensive enough to be useful. We suggest that you view these indicators as just about as likely to be relevant as those you would get from a consensus survey or from an untested theory; that is, as having a somewhat better chance of being relevant then ones developed in disregard of all three—research, general consensus, and theory. They are likely, however, to have the advantage that they suggest distinctions between classes of behavior which are not usually made. Also, they may suggest concepts or dimensions of behavior which are not common but may be useful. One of the outcomes of research, after all, is knowledge of what to measure and how to measure it.

One instrument exists which was constructed on just this principle: *Classroom Observations Keyed for Effectiveness Research* or COKER (Coker and Coker, 1979; also see Appendix E). We have already referred to a project in which an attempt was made to measure teacher effectiveness by deriving behavioral indicators from a local consensus and then using existing instruments to measure them (Medley et al., 1981). After the project was complete, those items on each instrument which had been included in behavioral indicators later found to relate to pupil learning outcomes (in this one study) were rewritten and assembled into a single new instrument, the COKER.

This approach yielded an instrument which contained specific items of behavior that not only *looked* relevant (because they had originally come from a consensus list) but also had a somewhat better-than-average chance of *being* relevant, because some empirical evidence that each one was valid had been obtained in at least one study.

If you decide to define your behavioral indicators with this sort of research base, you may find Appendix A helpful. This appendix summarizes the findings of the process-product research in 44 tables. The tables come from the report already mentioned (Medley, 1977) updated to include a few additional findings reported since the publication of the original monograph. What the 44 tables display are more than 600 significant relationships found between specific items of classroom behavior (miscalled competencies in the report) and pupil learning.

The tables are arranged so that similar behaviors tend to appear in the same table. The first step in using the table is to determine whether the item in question (or some item very similar to it) appears in one of the tables. If the item is shown, then its relationship to pupil learning is shown by grade level and socioeconomic status of the pupil, as well as by subject (reading or arithmetic) and by the level of measurement used in the study.

Each relationship found is reported separately as *H* (if the frequency of the behavior is *higher* in the classrooms of more effective teachers than in those of less effective teachers), as *L* (if the reverse is true) or as *M* (if the frequency of the behavior in the more effective teachers' classrooms is somewhere in the middle, and its frequency could be either high or low in the ineffective teachers' classrooms).

Each of these relationships was found in a methodologically sound study and was not only statistically significant (at the .05 level) but also large enough (greater than .39 in size) to be practically significant. As you will discover, few of the relationships have been verified, that is, found in two or more different studies; for this reason we regard most of them as tentative.

Perhaps the best way to use these tables is the way the Cokers used the findings of their study—that is, as a means of checking up on a set of specifications or list of behavior items derived either from a consensus survey or from a theoretical position. When you have arrived at a provisional list of the behaviors you wish to record by either of these two methods, you should check to see whether anyone has ever found a correlation between each specific item of behavior on your list and pupil learning, using teachers like those you propose to evaluate and pupils of the kind you will observe them teaching.

A search of the tables may support the use of an item, in which case you can retain it with increased confidence that it will work. Or it may not support the use of the item; in such a case you may find a similar item in one of the tables which you can use instead. If not, whether you retain the item or not will depend on how many indicators you have of the dimension it would be used to measure. If you are short of items, you might as well keep it and see how it works.

There may be cases in which an item which theory or expert opinion indicates should be positively related to outcomes appears in one of the tables to be negatively related. We suggest you retain such items as relevant, and decide how to weight them later.

Remember that, according to the theory of statistical inference, 95 percent of these findings would be verified if the study that produced them were repeated, so an instrument based on a set of items chosen in this way has an excellent chance of being a valid one.

One of the things you will notice as you study the tables is that in many cases the item of interest will have been found to be valid at one grade or socioeconomic level, or in one subject, but not others; that in some cases there is a reversal of the relationship from one grade level, subject or socioeconomic level to another. This does not pose a problem even if the contemplated instrument is to be used in any grade or subject or at any socioeconomic status level. Our concern here is that the item be relevant. If it proves necessary to develop different scoring keys for teachers of different grades, subject, or kinds of pupils, you can do so later.

SUMMARY

The first step in the development of a program for the measurement-based evaluation of teacher performance is the identification of the set of dimensions of teacher performance, a set of summary measures, and a set of specific items of behavior to be used as the basis for scoring performance on the dimensions identified. Once this step has been completed, it is possible to examine existing, well-established observation systems to determine which (if any) of them can be adopted or most readily adapted for use in the program. This determination should be based on an examination of the items or categories of behavior that can be found on a record made with the instrument, not on the dimensions presently measured with it, since new scoring keys for the instruments can be developed as needed by methods to be described in Chapter 8. If no existing system can be adopted or adapted, the specific items of behavior must be used as the starting point for developing a new instrument.

Three strategies for developing such a set of specifications are described: one based on theory, one on consensus about the nature of effective teaching, and one based on findings from the process-product research. It is recommended that a tentative set of behavior items be developed from theory or consensus, and then checked against the tables presented in Appendix A to see whether there is empirical support for the relevance of each item. The surviving set of items should possess face validity and should also be likely to provide the base for valid measures of effective teacher performance.

BIBLIOGRAPHY

Barr, A. S., B. V. Bechdolt, W. W. Coxe, N. L. Gage, J. S. Orleans, H. H. Renmers, and D. G. Ryans. "Report of the Committee on the Criteria of Teacher Effectiveness." *Review of Educational Research*, 1952, 22, 238–263.

Brown, B. B. "Experimentalism in Teaching Practice." *Journal of Research and Development in Education*, 1970, 4, 14–22.

Charters, W. W., and Douglas Waples. *The Commonwealth Teacher-Training Study*. Chicago: University of Chicago Press, 1929.

Coker, Homer, and Joan G. Coker. *Classroom Observations Keyed for Effectiveness Research—Observer Training Manual*. Atlanta, GA: Georgia State University/ Carroll County Teacher Corps Project, 1979.

Coker, Homer, Donald M. Medley, and Robert S. Soar. "How Valid Are Expert Opinions about Effective Teaching?" *Phi Delta Kappan*, 1980, 62, 131–134; 149.

Florida Catalog of Teacher Competencies. Tallahassee, FL: Florida Department of Education, 1973.

Jackson, P. W. *The Way Teaching Is*. Washington, DC: Association for Supervision and Curriculum Development and the National Education Association, 1966.

Johnson, C. E., J. R. Okey, W. Capie, C. Ellett, and P. T. Adams. *Identifying and Verifying Generic Teacher Competencies*. Athens, GA: College of Education, University of Georgia, 1978.

Joyce, B., and M. Weil. *Models of Teaching*. 2d ed. Englewood Cliffs, NJ: Prentice Hall, 1980.

MacDonald, J. B., and R. R. Leeper, eds. *Theories of Instruction*. Washington, DC: Association for Supervision and Curriculum Development, 1965.

Medley, Donald M. *Observation Schedule and Record, Form 5V*. Charlottesville, VA: University of Virginia, School of Education, 1973.

—— *Teacher Competence and Teacher Effectiveness: A Review of Process-Product Research*. Washington, DC: American Association of Colleges for Teacher Education, 1977.

Medley, Donald M., Homer Coker, Joan G. Coker, Jeffery L. Lorentz, Robert S. Soar, and Robert L. Spaulding. "Assessing Teacher Performance from Observed Competency Indicators Defined by Classroom Teachers." *Journal of Educational Research*, 1981, 74, 197–216.

Ryans, David G. *Characteristics of Teachers: Their Description, Comparison, and Appraisal*. Washington, DC: American Council on Education, 1960.

Smith, B. Othanel. *Teachers for the Real World*. Washington, DC: American Association of Colleges for Teacher Education, 1969.

Soar, R. L., R. M. Soar, and M. Rogosta. *Florida Climate and Control System (FLACCS): Observer's Manual*. Gainesville, FL: Institute for the Department of Human Resources, University of Florida, 1971.

Spaulding, Robert L. *Classroom Behavior Analysis and Treatment*. Durham, NC: Education Improvement Program, Duke University, 1969.

—— *Spaulding Teacher Activity Recording Schedule (STARS)*. San Jose, CA: San Jose State University, 1970.

Stiles, L. J., ed. *Theories for Teaching*. New York: Dodd, Mead, 1974.

Thomas, Lewis. "The Professional is Vulnerable to Fads—Medicine without Science." *The Atlantic Monthly*, April, 1981, 40–42.

Turner, R. L., ed. *A General Catalog of Teaching Skills*. Syracuse, NY: National Discrimination Center, Syracuse University, School of Education, n.d.

5

Structured Observation Systems

Once you have a clear specification of the behaviors upon which your evaluations of teachers are to be based you are ready to face the problem of adopting, adapting, or constructing an observation instrument, or perhaps more than one, with which to collect evaluative data. In this chapter we propose to discuss briefly the principal alternatives to structured observation systems and why none of these alternatives is suitable for this purpose. Then we will describe each of the major types of structured observation systems in use today, and an example of each. Finally we will say something about the problems you will face should you decide to construct your own instrument instead of adopting or adapting an existing system to your purposes.

ALTERNATIVES TO STRUCTURED OBSERVATION SYSTEMS

Before beginning to talk about structured observation systems in any detail, let us briefly compare them with some other systematic approaches to classroom observation. All of the approaches we shall consider were designed to help us obtain an accurate picture of what goes on in the classroom for one of two main purposes. Some observations are made for research purposes, to add to our knowledge of teaching and learning. Others are made for evaluative purposes, to support decisions about teachers, methods, curricula, etc. In this volume we are of course interested in observing classroom behavior for the purpose of evaluating the competence of the teachers whose performance we observe.

Let us consider briefly how ethnographic and ecological observations and supervisory ratings differ from observations made with a structured observation system.

A *structured observation system* consists essentially of a list of items or categories of behavior: the observer using such a system limits his observations to the listed items or categories of behaviors only, ignoring all other behaviors (except to the degree that they assist him in recording occurrences of the specified items).

The term *ecological observations* will be used here to refer to observations made without any such specifications; ecological observations are intended to be as exhaustive or complete as possible. The ecological observer aspires to record everything that happens without preconceptions about what is important. Categories of behavior may be used in interpreting or scoring an ecological record, but if so they are determined ex post facto. Ecological records can be and in fact have been made with a videotape recorder taking the place of the human observer.

The term *ethnographic observations* refers to observations also made without previous specification of what behaviors are to be attended to, but which focus particularly upon what is unique to the situation in which the observations are made, and which seek to capitalize on the sensitivity of the trained ethnographic observer to the phenomena being observed.

The term *rating scale* refers to an observation system which (1) specifies the *kinds* of behaviors the observer is to attend to in advance, but does not limit him to any specific behaviors; and (2) requires the observer to record not what he sees, but his *evaluation* of what he sees, in the form of numbers on a scale or dimension of performance specified before hand.

An ecological record is more objective than an ethnographic record, but because of the wealth of detail it contains (much of which will be irrelevant) quantifying such a record is too cumbersome and expensive a process to be practicable for routine use in teacher evaluation.

The ethnographic record is (1) too subjective, (2) too difficult to quantify, and (3) too dependent for its validity upon the expertise of the individual observer to be useful in routine teacher evaluations. The expertise required of the observer includes not only an extensive knowledge of pedagogy but also a high level of skill in ethnography, a level of skill very few practicing educators can be expected to acquire.

Supervisory ratings are better adapted to the routine evaluation of teaching than either of these other systems, but they too have important limitations. These limitations relate to the differences in the way that rating scales are expected to function from the way in which systematic observations are.

A teacher rating scale is (or ought to be) designed to assist the rater in making accurate judgments about the placement of the teacher on each of the dimensions to be rated. This is usually done by providing as clear a definition as possible not only of the dimension itself, but also of the kind of teacher performance that is typical of certain points on that scale or dimension. Most modern rating scales do this by providing thumbnail descriptions of the behaviors of teachers who should be rated at each extreme of the scale, and (perhaps) at one or more intermediate points. The rater can then compare the behaviors he observes on a visit with these descriptions and so locate the teacher on the scale.

A structured observation system, on the other hand, is designed to assist the recorder in observing and recording which of a predetermined set of behaviors occur during a visit and, in most cases, how often. It does this primarily by specifying what those behaviors are and providing a convenient means for recording their occurrence.

When a rating scale lists behaviors representing one or another level of performance along a dimension, the behaviors listed are regarded as typical or illustrative only. The rater is not expected to look for these specific behaviors alone, but for any behaviors he judges to be similar to them; and he is not expected to record which of the behaviors he observes.

It should be noted that it is critical that the rater know what dimension he is supposed to evaluate, what it means and what kinds of behaviors characterize different levels of the dimension. The behaviors themselves play a secondary role. The recorder, on the other hand, need not know what dimensions of teacher performance are being evaluated, or which of the behaviors he records are relevant to what dimensions, much less what level any particular behavior represents. Nor need he be concerned with judging what behaviors are similar to those listed. What it is critical for the observer to be able to do is to recognize a behavior when he sees it happen, nothing more.

One important implication of this is that the accuracy of ratings depends very much on the rater's knowledge of pedagogy and on his ability to grasp the meaning of each dimension in behavioral terms. The rater's ability to recognize which behaviors are similar enough to those cited as typical of a certain level of performance to be equivalent to them is crucial. For this reason, only the most highly trained and experienced educators can be expected to make valid ratings. One cannot train a relatively naive person to be a rater. Even beyond this, however, there is evidence to question whether even the most skilled observers are able to assemble bits of behavior into measures which are internally consistent on a rational basis (see Chapter 8).

The accuracy of a record made on an observation schedule, on the other hand, does not depend at all on the recorder's knowledge of pedagogy. It depends only on his ability to recognize the behaviors specified by the schedule. It is perfectly feasible to train any reasonably intelligent person to use an observation schedule, however naive he may be about the teaching process. And his records may be expected to be just as accurate as those of the most experienced and sophisticated professional educator.

Any attempt to evaluate teaching must use the judgments of experts at some point. Where systematic observation differs from teacher rating has to do with when and how the judgments are applied. In the case of ratings the expert judge must himself visit the classroom, observe the teacher's behavior, and make his judgments on the spot. In the case of systematic observations, the expert judgments are applied to a record of the behavior made by someone else, someone expert in recording behavior rather than in judging its meaning. These judgments are made independently of what goes on in any one classroom and are incorporated into a scoring key which is therefore applied with complete impartiality.

The record of behavior to which the judgments are applied when the record is scored is much less rich in detail than the behavior itself: a behavior record contains a highly simplified or abstracted version of what actually occurred. The art of constructing an observation system lies in ensuring that all or most of the details that are left out are irrelevant and that the details recorded contain an amount of relevant information that is sufficient for the purpose.

The analogy to achievement testing is close and instructive. We are accustomed to assessing a student's knowledge of some subject such as general science or modern history by giving him a test containing perhaps 50 multiple-choice items (or maybe 10 essay questions). In doing so we sacrifice a vast amount of detail about the student's knowledge of the subject, but if the items adequately sample the field, we do get an estimate of each student's knowledge that is accurate enough for most purposes. In fact, because of its objectivity, it usually gives a more accurate measure than we can obtain in any other way.

In assessing dimensions of teacher performance by structured observation we do much the same thing; we select a relatively small set of behaviors from all the relevant behaviors and base our assessment on them. The assessments we obtain are comparable in objectivity and reliability to scores on objective tests.

The preference most educators show for rating scales reflects a widely shared misunderstanding of the potential of structured observation systems. Most educators are unfamiliar with the more sophisticated systems available today and dismiss them on the grounds that since they are based on minute, even trivial, details of classroom behavior, the information they yield must also be trivial.

Nothing could be farther from the truth. As we shall try to illustrate in the pages to follow, a well-constructed system can yield measurements of major dimensions of classroom behavior that are more objective, reliable, and valid than any ratings and can illuminate the structure of effective teaching in a way that no subjective rating can, however expert the rater. When records made by skilled though pedagogically naive observers are used to extract information about teacher performance, insights and relationships of which the observers are totally unaware emerge. And this is accomplished without losing one bit of the objectivity of the records in the process. The examples to follow represent some of the most advanced applications of the measurement of human behavior that have yet appeared.

The structured observation schedule seems to combine the objectivity of the ecological record with the convenience and efficiency of the rating scale without requiring of its observers anything like the expertise required by ethnographic observers or raters. If we are wise enough in identifying the behaviors to be recorded we can secure as much of the relevant information an ecological record would contain as we need. If our scoring keys are wisely constructed we can reap as much of the benefit of the human sensitivity we would get if we used ethnographic observers or rating scales. And there are unique advantages growing out of the greater objectivity and detail achievable in such records which make them uniquely adapted to teacher evaluation. These advantages can be achieved only with considerable advance expenditure of time and effort; but they are worth it.

TYPES OF STRUCTURED OBSERVATION SYSTEMS

Three basic types of observation systems that we will refer to collectively as structured observation systems have evolved over the years: category systems, sign systems, and multiple coding systems. In the next few pages we shall describe in some detail an example of each kind of system.

A Category System

Perhaps the most familiar of the three approaches to structured observation is the *category system*. This is a set of behavior items or categories defined broadly enough so that any behavior in the domain to be observed can be recognized as an instance of one or another of them. The number of categories must be small enough so that the observer can remember them well enough to code them as they occur. As an example, Figure 5.1 shows the 10 items or categories which make up the Flanders system, *Interaction Analysis* (Flanders, 1970), a system

Teacher talk	1.	*Accepts feeling:* Accepts and clarifies the feeling tone of the students in a nonthreatening manner. Feelings may be positive or negative. Predicting or recalling feelings is included.
	2.	*Praises or encourages:* Praises or encourages student action or behavior. Jokes that release tension, but not at the expense of another individual; nodding head, or saying "um hm?" or "go on" are included.
Indirect influence	3.	*Accepts or uses ideas of students:* Clarifies, builds, or develops ideas suggested by a student. As teacher brings more of his own ideas into play, shift to category 5.
	4.	*Asks questions:* Asks a question about content or procedure with the intent that a student answer.
Direct influence	5.	*Lecturing:* Gives facts or opinions about content or procedures; expresses her own ideas, asks rhetorical questions.
	6.	*Giving directions:* directions, commands, or orders with which a student is expected to comply.
	7.	*Criticizing or justifying authority:* Statements intended to change student behavior from nonacceptable to acceptable pattern; bawling someone out; stating why the teacher is doing what she is doing; extreme self-reference.
Student talk	8.	*Student talk—response:* Talk by students in response to teacher. Teacher initiates the contact or solicits student statement.
	9.	*Student talk—initiation:* Talk by students which they initiate. If "calling on" student is only to indicate who may talk next, observer must decide whether student wanted to talk. If he did, use this category.
	10.	*Silence or confusion:* Pauses, short periods of silence, and periods of confusion in which communication cannot be understood by the observer.

FIGURE 5.1 Summary of categories for interaction analysis. (The numbers imply no scale, but are classificatory and designate a particular kind of communication event. Writing down the numbers during observation is to enumerate not to judge a position on a scale.)

which has had a major influence on the field of systematic observation
and has almost certainly been used by more investigators than any other
system.*

The central distinction on which the rationale of this system is based
is between two different types of influence used by a teacher in verbal
interaction with pupils. *Direct teacher influence* refers to a one-way style of
communication in which the teacher gives information and directions
and expects pupils to follow them. *Indirect teacher influence* refers to a
style which permits pupils to have input into the direction and content
of the discussion, and in which the teacher accepts or uses at least some
of the ideas they suggest. The teacher exerts her influence by deciding
which ideas will be accepted and which will be encouraged by extension
or expansion.

The ten categories of verbal behavior which make up the system are
shown in Figure 5.1. Categories 1 through 4 are identified as forms of
indirect teacher influence, and categories 5 through 7 as forms of direct
influence. There are also two categories for pupil talk: a relatively
narrow, direct pupil response to a teacher question is classified in
category 8; any idea or a question proposed by a pupil which is not
narrowly responsive to a teacher's question is classified in category 9.

The observer using Flanders' system records the category number
that describes what is occurring every three seconds (unless what is
happening changes within three seconds, in which case numbers
representing the changes are recorded in sequence). An example of a
short segment of interaction is presented in Figure 5.2, along with the
codes.

Notice that the question with which the teacher opened this segment of discussion took more than three seconds, so category 4 was
recorded twice. This occurrence of the same code twice in sequence has
particular meaning, as we will indicate later. Jim's answer to the
teacher's question was coded 9 since the question was a broad one (it
would not have been possible to have said what a right or wrong answer
would be before the pupil spoke). The teacher's response to Jim ended
up as a question, but it was a question which invited an expansion of the
idea he suggested, so it was coded 3 rather than 4. Had it been a new
question by the teacher, it would have been coded a 4. Paul and Jane
built on Jim's idea, and since the thoughts were initiated by pupils they
were coded 9; and Jane's remark was long enough so that it received two
codes. The teacher's response to Jane was in effect a summary of what
had been said, and permitted the idea to remain in discussion for further
elaboration, so it was also coded a 3. Tom continued to build on the idea,

* The discussion of the Flanders system has been adopted from a presentation in Soar
and Soar (1982) with the permission of the publisher.

Speaker	Utterance	Code
T	What if Columbus hadn't lived—(pause)—what do you suppose would have happened to our country?	(4,4)
JIM	I think someone else would have discovered us.	(9)
T	Jim thinks someone else would have discovered us—what do others think?	(3)
PAUL	I don't see why. Columbus was very unusual.	(9) (10)
JANE	But, spices cost a lot—and people wanted a better way to get them from India.	(9,9)
T	So there was a lot of interest in trade with India—	(3)
TOM	Yes, and lots of other people were sailing long distances about then.	(9)
T	I think we also have to think about who would have supplied the ships and men for such a trip (pause). You know Isabella's husband, the king, wasn't enthusiastic.	(5,5)

FIGURE 5.2   An example of coding with interaction analysis.

so another 9 was recorded. But notice the effect of the final teacher statement. Rather than continuing with ideas which pupils have introduced, the teacher introduced an idea of her own which had the potential of taking the discussion in a different direction. Since this idea was the teacher's, it was coded 5. Because the teacher brought in a new idea, the stream of development to which several pupils have contributed up to this point was likely to be terminated.

To facilitate interpretation of the interaction these numbers are tabulated in a matrix. Putting a record into this form enables us to use one step of sequence in interpreting and scoring the record. The process is illustrated in Figure 5.3. The sequence of numbers which represents the interaction in Figure 5.2 is shown at the left of Figure 5.3 under the heading *Pairs of Codes*. In preparation for tallying them, the categories have been marked off in successive pairs. Note that the second number of the first pair becomes the first number of the second pair, and so on.

Each pair is then tallied into the matrix. The first number of each pair is taken as the number of the row and the second as the number of

PAIRS OF
CODES

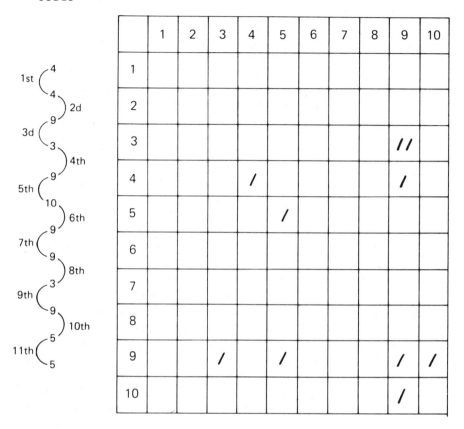

FIGURE 5.3   An example of an interaction analysis matrix.

the column in which the pair is tallied. Thus the 4/4 pair is recorded by
reading across row 4 to column 4 and entering a tally; the 4/9 pair is
tabulated by reading across row 4 and entering a tally in column 9; and
so on. Every cell in the matrix now represents an interaction in which
the row is the first part and column is the second part. These interactions are the primary items used in interpreting and scoring the record.

We can infer a number of things about this brief segment of
interaction from the matrix. On one occasion the teacher asked a
question (her own idea) which lasted more than three seconds (the 4/4
cell).

On another occasion she asked a question which was briefer, but
which was followed by a pupil response in which a correct answer could
not be predicted, so presumably the question was a broad one (4/9).
Although it is by no means certain, the inference is that both tallies

represent broad questions, since a factual question is likely to be brief and is likely to be followed by an 8 rather than a 9.

Three tallies fall in cells for which the row and column number are the same (4/4, 5/5, and 9/9). Since any activity must continue for more than three seconds in order for the row and column number to be the same, the implication is that the interaction was relatively leisurely.

All of the pupil tallies are 9s and none are 8s, which further supports the idea that pupils are contributing ideas on their own, rather than responding with right or wrong answers to narrow questions. The entire set of tallies suggests a pattern of interaction in which relatively broad ideas are being explored, pupils are contributing ideas of their own, the teacher is inviting further elaboration of pupils' ideas, and the process takes place in leisurely fashion. If a similar pattern were found in a matrix based on a larger number of tallies, we would of course have more confidence in our inferences.

What would you expect a matrix recorded during a drill session or a rapid-fire recitation to look like? Would you expect to see 3s or 4s? Would you expect to see more 8s or 9s? Would you expect to see two 9s in succession? Wouldn't you expect, if the interaction were rapid fire, if all the questions were factual, and if the teacher indicated the correctness of the response by asking another question, that a major proportion of the tallies would be in two cells, 4/8 and 8/4? There might be some deviations from this pattern, as when a pupil answered incorrectly or a pupil asked a question, but most of the tallies would fall into these two cells.

What would a matrix recorded while a teacher is having management problems look like? If the teacher criticized a pupil, implying he should not have done what he did, where would that go? If the teacher gave directions in order to correct the behavior and say what should be done next, where would that tally go? If the teacher scolded a child at some length (more than three seconds) in which cell of the matrix would that tally appear? If the teacher gave extended directions—directions lasting more than three seconds—where would that go? It should be clear that a build up in cells represented by the intersection of rows and columns 6 and 7 would represent management difficulties, and that a build up in the 7/7 cell would indicate extended criticism by the teacher.

Which cells (or cell) would you expect to show a high frequency if a teacher typically responded to pupils' ideas by accepting or using them rather than by bringing in ideas of her own? One thing you would be looking for is teacher talk; in what category or categories? Since you would be looking for teacher talk which followed pupil talk, you would be looking in the rows with which numbers? What category of pupil talk would you look for? And since the pupil talk is to represent ideas initiated by the pupil, rather than responses to teacher questions, what particular row would you look at? Teacher responses will be tallied in columns 1 through 7; among these, columns 2 and 3 in particular will reflect responses which accept or build on pupil ideas, while columns 4 and 5 will reflect teacher ideas. The row which reflects pupil ideas is row 9. So the relative numbers of tallies in 9/2 and 9/3 as compared with 9/4 and 9/5 would reflect the relative number of teacher responses that accept and build on pupil ideas in contrast to those which terminate the pupil thought and begin an idea of the teacher's.

The foregoing discussion should give you some idea of the use this sophisticated category system makes of sequence of events. The second tally in each pair tells us something about the first and the first tells us something about the second, so that by interpreting categories in pairs we learn much more than we could ever learn by looking only at single categories.

The fact that the observer uses only 10 categories to record the behavior makes it relatively easy to train observers to code accurately; this is one reason why this kind of a record is so much more objective than a set of ratings. The decisions or inferences that the recorder must make to decide which number to write down are much easier to make than those a rater must make before writing down his number, and whether that number is correct depends much less on the professional expertise of the recorder than the accuracy of a rating depends on the professional expertise of the rater.

The fact that 100 cell frequencies (10 × 10) are available for use in interpreting or scoring the record permits the interpreter or scorer to draw inferences from a record that are comparable in sophistication to those drawn by the rater, but do not depend on inferences made by the observer under time pressure and other kinds of stress.

You should understand that in practice we avoid drawing inferences from matrices based on such brief samples of interaction as that used as an example. The fact that this observed matrix suggested a certain kind of teacher remains a suggestion until a sample of interaction has been recorded which is long enough to establish that the pattern is stable and reliable.

A Sign System

A second type of structured observation that has been widely used— though not, perhaps as widely as category systems have—is the *sign system*.

Instead of a set of categories into one of which any behavior must be classifiable a sign system is a list of rather narrowly defined behaviors called signs, each of which is considered relevant to a dimension of behavior that is to be measured. If the observer sees one of the listed

Teacher_____Sch._____Gr._____Subj._____Obs._____Date_____Time_____

		CONTEXT					
		T. Init./ P. Responds Pupil		Follow-up Pupil		P. Initiates T. Responds Pupil	
		Dis-obey	Other	Inapp.	Other	Inapp.	Dev. Act.	Other
Teacher Control		01	02	03	04	05	06	07
10 Acknowledges, Agrees, Complies								
11 Praises (SM)								
12 Asks for status								
13 Suggests, guides								
14 Feedback, cites reason								
15 Correct w/o criticism (SM)								
16 Questions for control								
17 Ques., states behav. rule								
18 Directs with reason								
19 Directs w/o reason								
20 Uses time pressure								
21 Reminds, Prods								
22 Interrupts, cuts off								
23 Supv. P. closely, immobilizes								
24 Criticizes, warns (SM)								
25 Orders, commands								
26 Scolds, punishes								
27 Nods, smiles, facial feed bk.								
28 Uses "body English", waits								
29 Gestures								
30 Touches, pats								
31 Shakes head, eye contact								
32 Takes equipment, book								

33 Signals, raps									
34 Glares, frowns									
35 Holds, pushes, spanks									
36 Ignores, abandons									
37 Involvement		▓		▓			▓		

Groupings	*Rewards*	*Pupil Behaviors*
41 T. not available	56 Gives, promises, reward	73 Task related movement
42 Pupil as individual	57 Praises behavior—spec	74 Flw routine w/o remind
43 Total group w teacher	58 Praises work—spec	75 Aimless wandering
44 Small group w teacher	59 Praises, General, Ind.	76 Asks permission
45 Individual w teacher	60 Praises, General, Grp.	77 Reports rule another
46 Structured group w/o T		78 Tattles
47 Free groups	*Pupil Work*	79 Shows bravado
	61 Pupil Central	80 Gives reason, direction
Teacher	62 Pupil—no choice	81 Speaks aloud w/o permis.
48 Teacher central	63 Pupil—limited choice	82 Seeks reassurance supp.
49 Moves freely among P	64 Pupil—free choice	83 Shows pride
50 Teacher orients	65 (Seat work w/o teacher	84 Shows fear, shame, hemil
51 Uses Surrogate blkbd/av	66 (Seat work with teacher	85 Shows apathy
52 Attends pupil briefly	67 (Works w/ much superv.	
53 Attends pupil closely	68 (Works w/ little superv.	*Socialization*
54 Attends P in succession	69 Work with socializ	86 Almost never
55 Attends simultan. activ.	70 Cooperative work	87 Occasionally
	71 Collaborative work	88 Frequently
	72 Competitive work	
		P. Int.-Att. to Task
		89 (Rank 1 low to 5 high)

FIGURE 5.4 The first page of the *Climate and Control System*. (From Soar and Soar, 1982.)

behaviors occur, he records the fact. If he sees any behavior not on his list occur he ignores it.

Each observation session is divided into short periods, usually between two and five minutes long. During each period the observer is expected to record which of the listed behaviors he observed during that period *but not how often*. Information about the relative frequency of a behavior is based on the number of periods during an observation in which the behavior was observed, rather than on how often it was observed during any one period.

Since the observer using a sign system does not have to code and record every event that occurs, his task is easier than that of an observer using a category system and it is possible to include more items covering a greater range of behaviors, such as both verbal and nonverbal behaviors, groupings, movement, etc. This makes it possible for a record made on a sign system to contain details not available in a record made on a category system.

As an example of a sign system we shall use the *Climate and Control System* (CCS; Soar and Soar, 1982).

As the name implies, this system is used to record teacher management behavior, pupil responses to it, and expressions of affect by both teachers and pupils. A copy of the first page, on which management behavior is recorded, is shown in Figure 5.4. The upper portion of the page is a matrix which the observer uses to record sequences of interaction between teacher and pupils. The column heads indicate three contexts within which pupil behavior occurs: (1) pupil response to an initiation made by the teacher (columns 1 and 2); (2) pupil behavior in the context of continuing interaction between the teacher and a particular subgroup (columns 3 and 4); and (3) initiations or behaviors by pupils not in the group with whom the teacher is currently interacting to which the teacher responds (columns 5 through 7). Within each of the first two contexts the observer codes and records pupil behavior either as *inappropriate* (disobeys) or as *other* (which commonly means *appropriate*). In the third context, pupil behavior may also be coded and recorded as *deviant, active*.

The rows in the matrix represent teacher behaviors designed either to modify the behavior of a pupil or to maintain an activity already under way. Items 10 through 26 are verbal behaviors, 27 through 37 are nonverbal behaviors. Each of these two sets of teacher behaviors is roughly scaled from the uncoercive, unobtrusive behaviors recorded at the top end of the scale, to the relatively harsh, obtrusive behaviors recorded at the bottom of the set. Let us consider some examples.

1.   If, while the teacher is working with a reading group, a pupil doing seat work brings his work to her for help, and the teacher gives

the help, that interaction would be recorded in row 10, column 7. Column 7 is used because the pupil was not a part of the group with whom the teacher was working and because he approached the teacher appropriately. Row 10 was used because the teacher met his request.

2. If the teacher, in the course of walking around the classroom, calls to the classroom as a whole, "How many are finished with arithmetic?" and some pupils respond by putting up hands, that would be recorded at 12/02. The teacher *asks for status* (row 12) and the pupils comply by giving information (column 2). (This is seen by the observer as management behavior because in addition to giving the teacher information, it also gave information to the straggling pupils and urged them on by helping them discover that they were straggling.) Some teachers keep their classrooms together and moving almost entirely through the use of this one tactic.

3. If the teacher looked up to a child at the side of the room and asked, "John, would you shut the door, please?" that would be an example of 13 *suggest, guides*. (It is a clear direction, but it is softened by a please and it comes in the form of a question.) If the child complied, the event would be recorded at 13/02.

4. If two pupils were nudging, punching, and pushing each other and the teacher said to one of them, "Jim, I think there's room for you here by me," and waited until the child came to sit by her, that would be recorded at 14/05 to indicate that a child outside the group with whom the teacher is working was engaging in inappropriate behavior and the teacher responded with feedback.

5. If the teacher directed a question to a pupil in the group with which she was interacting who was inattentive, and the need to answer the question brought the pupil back on task, that would be recorded at 16/04, reflecting the fact that, during a continuing interaction between the teacher and the group the teacher addressed a subject matter question to an off-task pupil with management intact and that the pupil responded appropriately.

To the degree that the interactions recorded appear toward the top of either list, we may infer that the teacher's style tends to be unobtrusive and less authority laden; that is, to be based more on giving feedback to children on the appropriateness of their behavior then on the use of more direct or repressive means. Classrooms in which this is a pervasive style are likely to give the impression of running themselves, because the management behavior is not obvious and likely not to be noticed. On the other hand, matrices from classrooms where the teacher is visibly struggling to establish control by ordering, commanding, and criticizing are characterized by tallies mainly toward the lower level of

NEGATIVE AFFECT

Teacher Verbal

A 1	Says "stop it," etc.
A 2	Uses sharp tone
A 3	Rejects child
A 4	Criticizes, blames, warns
A 5	Sounds defensive
A 6	Yells
A 7	Scolds, humiliates
A 8	Other
A 9	Code Involvement

Pupil Verbal

A10	Says "No," "I won't" etc.
A11	Teases
A12	Laughs
A13	Tattles
A14	Commands or demands
A15	Makes disparaging remark
A16	Demands attention
A17	Sounds defensive
A18	Finds fault
A19	Threatens
A20	Other
A21	Code involvement

Teacher Nonverbal

A22	Waits for child
A23	Frowns
A24	Points, shakes finger
A25	Pushes or pulls, holds
A26	Shows disgust
A27	Takes material
A28	Refuses to respond to child
A29	Other

Pupil Nonverbal

A30	Makes face, frowns
A31	Pouts, withdraws
A32	Uncooperative, resistant
A33	Stamps, throws, slams
A34	Interferes, threatens
A35	Takes, damages property
A36	Picks at child
A37	Pushes or pulls, holds
A38	Hits, hurts
A39	Is left out
A40	Other

POSITIVE AFFECT

Teacher Verbal		*Teacher Nonverbal*	
A41	Says, "Thank you," etc.	A62	Accepts favor for self
A42	Agrees with child	A63	Waits for child
A43	Supports child	A64	Gives individual attention
A44	Gives individual attention	A65	Warm, congenial
A45	Warm, congenial	A66	Listens carefully to child
A46	Praises child	A67	Smiles, laughs, nods
A47	Develops "we feeling"	A68	Pats, hugs, etc.
A48	Is enthusiastic	A69	Sympathetic
A49	Other	A70	Other
A50	Code Involvement		

Pupil Verbal		*Pupil Nonverbal*	
		A71	Helpful, shares
A51	Says "Thank you," etc.	A72	Leans close to another
A52	Sounds friendly	A73	Chooses another
A53	Agrees, peer support	A74	Smiles, laughs with another
A54	Initiates contact	A75	Pats, hugs another
A55	Offers to share, cooperate	A76	Agreeable, cooperative
A56	Banters	A77	Enthusiastic
A57	Is enthusiastic	A78	Horseplay
A58	Praises another	A79	Other
A59	Helps another		
A60	other		
A61	Code Involvement		

Code Involvement:

0. None involved   2. Up to one-half the class

1. Few involved   3. More than half

FIGURE 5.5   The second page of the *Climate and Control System*. (From Soar and Soar, 1982.)

either of the two item sets. To the extent that the tallies occur in the first two columns, the classroom activity is initiated and led by the teacher, and to the extent that those tallies are in column 2, the pupils are complying. If most of the tallies are in columns 5, 6, or 7, the teacher is behaving more often in a responding mode, dealing with behavior initiated by pupils, rather than organizing activities to which students are responding. Within these three columns of pupil initiation, there are three levels ranging from appropriate, complying behavior through inappropriate behavior to behavior which is actively disruptive.

Item sets at the bottom of the page, which are tallied at the end of the period, represent the nature of the groups that are present, whether pupils tend to work as individuals or in small groups, whether the teacher is with the individual or small group, whether the teacher sets up the groups or pupils are free to organize groups at their own volition (*groupings*). The extent to which the teacher is central to pupil activities, in contrast to moving around among pupils, and the closeness of attention given to individual pupils are represented in the blockheaded *teacher*. The specifics of the incentive system are indicated in the block *rewards*. *Pupil work* identifies the freedom of choice pupils have in their behavior, the extent to which the teacher is supervising them and/or available to them, and whether the work itself is competitive or cooperative. *Pupil behavior* records the responses of pupils to teacher management behavior, and the extent to which pupils take responsibility for the management of the classroom in contrast to creating management problems to which the teacher must respond. The degree of socialization is indicated in a block with that name. The final item on the page is used to record an estimate of the proportion of pupils in a classroom who appear to be working at some task. This simple estimate has been found to correlate well (high .70s) with scores based on more detailed systems for recording pupil on-task behavior (Ashton, Webb, and Doda, 1983).

The second page of the instrument, shown in Figure 5.5, is used to record expressions of affect in eight sets of items which represent the combinations of teacher versus pupil, positive versus negative and verbal versus nonverbal. It also provides for recording the proportion of pupils involved in each expression of affect, so that if all the teacher criticism (A4), for instance, is directed to one problem child, that situation can be distinguished from a situation in which the teacher criticizes many children.

To the reader inexperienced in the use of sign systems, learning to make accurate records with CCS (or any similar sign system) is likely to appear far more difficult than it is. The logical structure of the instrument and the way in which the items are arranged greatly reduce the role that rote memorization plays in the process. Learning the system is much more like concept learning than learning to use a category system;

one might say that what the recorder must learn is where to record a behavior, not how to code it.

The recorder's task is greatly facilitated by the strategy used, which is to record in the matrix during the period and to tally the other items immediately after the period ends and before beginning the next period of observation. The psychological set of the recorder should be quite different from that of the rater or the coder using a category system. His task is to record the range and variety of interactions that occur in three to five minutes, which tends to be less than you might imagine. Most of the things that happen, happen more than once, so that it is almost impossible to miss them (all you need do is see each of them once.) Things that happen less frequently tend to be conspicuous and difficult to miss. And the less frequent the event, the smaller the error of measurement that results if you fail to record it. Our own informal tests indicate that records made on sign systems tend to be more reliable than ones made on category systems when the items are the same.

Composite scores can be derived from sign records to score a variety of major dimensions of classroom behavior because of the number and variety of behavioral indicators that the records contain.

A Multiple Coding System

A third type of structured observation system will be referred to here as a *multiple coding system*, because the observer using such a system codes a single behavior or event on more than one category system. The use of such a system may involve event sampling: coding a single event in several category sets may take so much time that it is not possible to code every event that occurs in the busy classroom.

We shall discuss this kind of system in terms of an instrument called PROSE (Personal Record of School Experience; Medley, 1971). This instrument was originally designed to produce objective records of the experiences individual pupils have in school.

The observer using the system carries a cassette recorder loaded with a cassette that emits signals at preset time intervals. The basic interval is 20 seconds: at second 14 the tape emits the word *watch* and at second 20 the word *record* into an earplug worn by the observer. The observer has a previously prepared recording form for each pupil he is to observe. He locates the first pupil and observes him until he hears the word *record*, whereupon he describes what is happening to that child at that moment by marking the appropriate spaces on the instrument. He has 14 seconds in which to complete this task; when he finishes it (or when he hears *watch*) he agains focuses his attention on the target child. This process is repeated until five events have been recorded, at which time the recorder records "context" on the back of the recording form. Then he turns to the second form, locates the second child, and repeats the process with him. Depending on the purpose of the study the

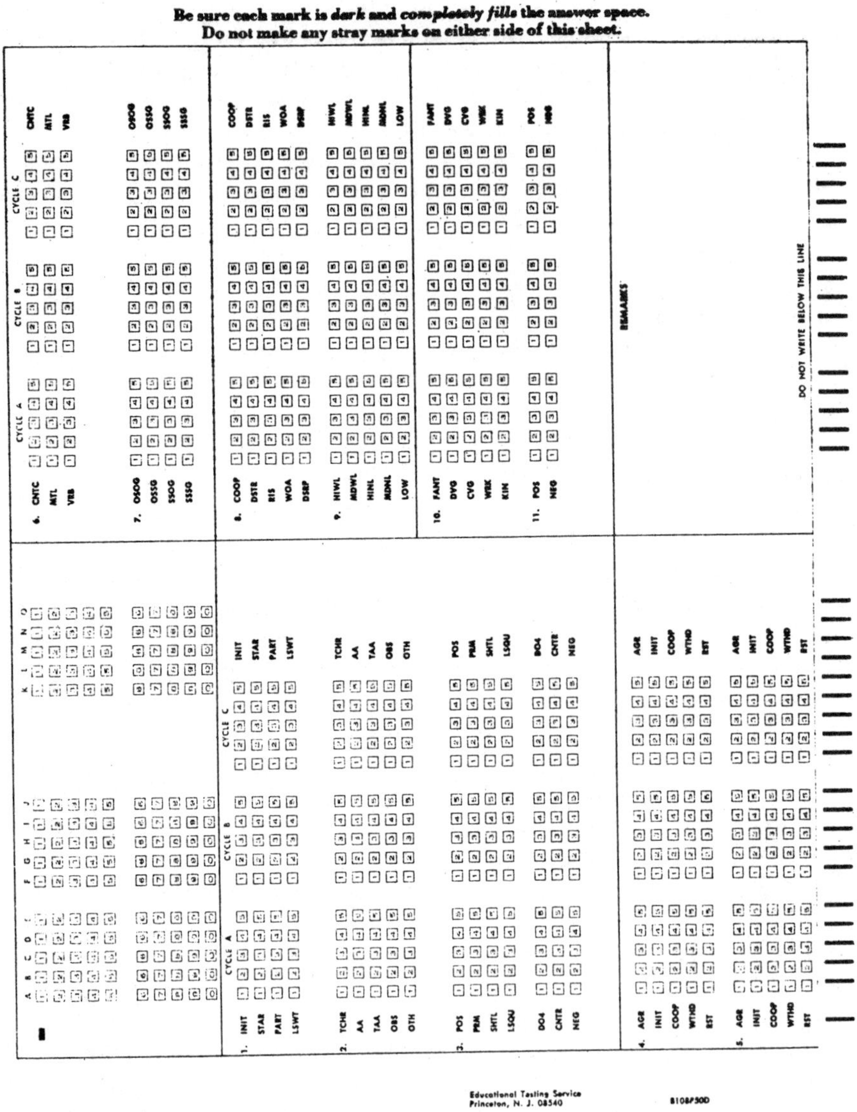
Be sure each mark is dark and completely fills the answer space.
Do not make any stray marks on either side of this sheet.
REMARKS
DO NOT WRITE BELOW THIS LINE
Educational Testing Service
Princeton, N. J. 08540
8108P50D

FIGURE 5.6 The statement side of PROSE. (From Medley, 1971.)

number of pupils observed and the number of experiences recorded per child may vary.

Figure 5.6 shows one side of the recording form. The first experience of the child observed is recorded in column 1, the second in column 2, and so on, until five events are recorded. This completes one cycle. Provision is made for recording three cycles of five experiences each; if more than 15 experiences per child are to be recorded, more than one form must be used for each child.

To illustrate how experiences are recorded, let us suppose that the observer is watching a child and that when he hears the word *record* the child is sitting in his seat in the middle of the class listening while the teacher is asking a question of another child. This experience will be described in terms of 11 items called *words*.

Word 1 is a four-category system: the categories clarify relationships between the child and the teacher (or other authority figure). In this instance, the child is attending to the teacher, but the teacher is not attending to him; so the recorder marks LSWT (listening/watching). If the teacher had been talking to the class or to a group of which the target child was a part, the recorder would have marked PART. If the teacher had been asking the target child a question, or in some other way singling him out (perhaps rebuking or praising him) he would have marked STAR. If the child had been asking a question or in some other fashion trying to get individual attention from the teacher, he would have marked INIT (initiating). If the child had not been in contact with the teacher or any authority figure—had been reading to himself, let us say—the recorder would have left this word blank.

Word 2 is used to identify the authority figure involved in the first item as either the teacher in charge of the class (TCHR), an adult teaching aid (AA), a teen-age aid (TAA), the observer (OBS), or some other adult such as a visiting parent (OTH). Again, if the child is not in contact with any authority figure the word is left blank. In our example, the recorder would, of course, mark TCHR.

Word 3 contains seven categories of communication from a teacher (or other authority figure) to a child: POS (positive affect), PRM (giving permission), SHTL (showing, demonstrating, telling), LSQU (listening or questioning), DO4 (doing something for the child that he would ordinarily do himself), CNTR (controlling), and NEG (negative affect). In our example the recorder would mark LSQU.

Words 4 and 5 would be left blank in our example, because they are marked only when the child is not in contact with an authority figure and is in contact with another child. Word 6 classifies communication according to the medium through which it takes place. In our example the recorder would mark VRB (verbal). If the communication had been through some material—if the teacher had been handing the child a book, for example—the recorder would mark MTL (material); if the contact had been physical—if, for instance, the teacher had been patting the child's head—he would mark CNTC (contact).

Word 7 is used to indicate the sex and ethnic mix in an interaction. Assuming that our teacher was female and our pupil male, the teacher would belong to the opposite sex. If both parties were members of the same ethnic group, the recorder would mark OSSG (opposite sex, same group).

Word 8 classifies the level of attention of the pupil to the task structured for him (in this case, listening to the teacher) in one of five categories. In our example the recorder would mark COOP (cooperating) because the pupil is doing what he is supposed to do. If instead he happened to be watching another pupil misbehave, the recorder would mark DSTR (distracted); if the pupil had been idly gazing out the window he would mark RIS (responding to internal stimuli); if the pupil had been surreptitiously doing his arithmetic the recorder would mark WOA (working on other activity); if the pupil had been preventing someone from paying attention he would mark DSRP (disruptive).

Word 9 is used to indicate the pupil's activity level—in this case, the recorder would mark LOW since the pupil is sitting quietly. Other options are HIWL (high with locomotion)—running around; MDWL (moderate with locomotion)—walking about; HINL (high, no locomotion)—bouncing up and down in his seat; and MDNL (moderate, no locomotion)—writing, manipulating tools, etc., in his seat.

Word 10 classifies the type of task the child is engaged in; in our example the recorder would mark CVG (convergent) because the task is defined *for* the pupil rather than *by* him. If the pupil had been finger painting or building something with blocks the recorder would mark DVG (divergent) because the nature of the task is defined by the pupil—he decides where to put his paint or his blocks next. If the pupil had been pretending to negotiate a toy truck through a town represented by blocks the recorder would mark FANT (fantasy). If the child had been putting away the toys or passing out the orange juice the recorder would mark WRK (work). If the child had been wandering aimlessly about or idly tapping one block on another the recorder would mark KIN (kinesthetic). As with all 11 words, the recorder has the option of leaving the word blank if what the child is doing does not fit any of these categories.

Word 11 would be left blank in our example because it is marked only when the child manifests affect. If the child had been crying, the recorder would have marked NEG (negative); if the child had been laughing, he would have marked POS (positive).

By the time the recorder finishes all 11 words the 14 seconds would have almost ended; in any case, he would start to watch the child again so that when he heard the next *record* he would know what was happening to the child.

A column which has been marked is referred to as a *statement* about that child's school experience. A record of a child's school experiences based on one or more cycles consists of 5 or more statements about the child's school experiences, each of which contains 11 words and each of which can be read by a computer. The computer, when properly programmed, can develop summary statements describing the child's school experiences, such as how often he was a STAR—how often the teacher (or a surrogate) recognized him as an individual person, what proportion of his time was spent sitting still and listening, how much positive affect the teacher displayed toward him, and so on.

Statements about the teacher can also be obtained from the computer, such as how often she asked questions of any child, how often she actually touched a child of the same or different sex or ethnic group; how much pupil movement she permitted, etc.

In a similar fashion, summary statements about the kinds of experiences pupils have in different classrooms or schools, under different curricula, in different subjects, and so on can be obtained from appropriate sets of records.

It has been mentioned that there are two sides to this instrument. After each five-statement cycle the observer turns the form over to the "context" side to record what was going on elsewhere in the classroom while the child was having the five experiences recorded. The overt instructional objectives; the roles played by the teacher and (if present) by the aide or aides; the materials used; the physical location of the child; and the general climate of the class during this period; all of these are recorded in addition to any of some 32 sign items observed to occur during the cycle.

This system is typical of multiple coding systems in that it produces relatively rich but lean data; that is, it yields much more detail about each experience than a simple category system would provide, but the number of experiences actually recorded tends to be smaller. In the case of PROSE, for example, more than two million different statements can be generated using the 11 available items. If context information is regarded as modifying the statement, then the number of different possible statements boggles the mind. But less than one experience is recorded per 20 seconds of observation.

SHOULD YOU BUILD YOUR OWN SYSTEM?

If you have trouble finding a systematic observation schedule (or two or three of them) that meets your needs, you may consider developing your own instrument. You will not be ready to make such a decision, of course, until you have read the rest of this book (particularly Chapters 4 and 8). But this seems to be a good place to discuss some of the issues you will face if you decide to go this route.

Developing a Category System

Most existing systems were originally built by researchers rather than by evaluators, and most of them chose to construct either a category system or a multiple coding system, rather than a sign system. But many of the factors that governed their choice are different from those that concern the educator seeking a better way to evaluate teacher performance. The researcher does not usually start out with a set of behavioral indicators that he wishes to observe; instead, he proceeds from a theoretical position which specifies a basis for a set of categories. A case in point is the hypothesis about direct and indirect teaching which led Flanders to develop the 10 categories described earlier in this chapter. Starting from such a framework can greatly accelerate the process of developing such a system. Even so, the process is a slow one and involves many tryouts and revisions before a really satisfactory set of categories can be developed. Most successful category systems in use today were at least 10 years in the making. Any instrument which is to be used to evaluate individual teachers and provide the information base for decisions that have momentous effects on their careers must meet standards of quality not achieved overnight. If you decide to build a category system of your own you must be prepared, then, for a long period of experimental use (which you may be able to shorten somewhat by obtaining expert assistance both in the initial steps and in the refinement phase as well), a period of definition, redefinition, and re-redefinition which may go on for months and even years.

Our own experience in evolving just the categories for teacher questions used with OScAR 5V may serve to illustrate this point, particularly since we did not proceed from any strong theoretical point of view. In our earliest attempts to measure teacher behavior we used a version of an earlier system that was simple almost to the point of elegance (in the mathematical sense): the Withall categories (Withall, 1949). The Withdall categories were, in fact, so simple that both questions and statements related to lesson content were coded in the same category, a category called *Problem Structuring*. By the time we began work on OScAR 3 we felt a need not only to distinguish questions from statements, but also to recognize that there are different kinds of questions that teachers ask.

We defined three categories of questions for OScAR 3: simple, complex, and affective-imaginative, and used them in a large-scale study of the behavior of student teachers (Medley and Mitzel, 1962). When we analyzed the data we found that our observers did not reliably distinguish complex questions from simple ones, and that they almost never recorded any affective-imaginative questions at all.

When we started work on OScAR 4V we obtained 50 kineoscope

recordings of student teachers in their classrooms, and spent many hours coding and recoding these films, using a series of revisions of OScAR 3. One of the first things we did was to try to identify some simple, clearly noticeable cues on the basis of which observers could consistently tell simple and complex questions apart. Eventually it became clear to us that the surest way to recognize a simple question was according to the kind of answer the teacher seemed to be seeking. Most of the time, when a teacher asks a question it is apparent that she has in mind the answer she wants to get; in other words, there is one and only one answer which will be accepted by the teacher as correct.

We wasted a lot of time, by the way, under the mistaken notion that a simple question would be one that called for a yes or no answer. Not so. A yes-no question can be phrased at any level of the Bloom taxonomy (with the possible exception of synthesis) (Bloom *et al.*, 1956).

What we eventually came to call a *convergent* question is a question which requires the pupil to emit the precise answer the teacher wants. This does not correspond perfectly to the lowest level of the Bloom taxonomy, which is what we originally meant by a simple question. Nor do *divergent* questions—ones which offer pupils a choice of acceptable answers, an opportunity to be original without being wrong—always fall at one of the highest levels of the taxonomy. But the difference between them seemed if anything a more important difference than the one between simple or lower-order questions and complex or higher-order questions that we originally sought.

The difference in the intellectual climate in a classroom where convergent questions predominate from that in one where divergent questions are common is critical. As John Holt points out, pupils in the convergent classroom learn not to think but to guess; school becomes a guessing game in which the pupil who tries to think what the correct answer is always loses because someone else will guess the answer before he figures it out (Holt, 1967). Convergent questions have a useful function in drill sessions; divergent ones appear in brainstorming sessions and in discussions in which creativity and originality are encouraged.

It is so easy to tell the two apart that almost anyone can learn to do so in a few minutes, or even a few seconds! Note that the distinction is very similar to that made by Flanders between pupils responses in categories 8 and 9; but we felt that the two were easier to distinguish on the basis of our cues than his.

But even before this insight came we began to sense that there was another kind of question just as important, and sometime after we defined the first two categories we identified a third. This was the kind of a question that was related to answers made to previous questions; a question, perhaps, that required the pupil to react to something he or someone else had already said. Such questions must be asked if pupils are to learn to see knowledge as structure rather than as a mere collection of facts and rules. Such questions must be asked if pupils are to learn to listen to one another—that is, to take part in genuine discussions (as distinguished from recitations). Such questions must be asked, finally, if pupils are expected to learn to think, to reflect, to evaluate, to generalize.

We called these questions *elaborating* questions for some years before a graduate assistant pointed out that there are in reality two very different kinds of elaborating questions. One kind, the kind we called *elaborating 1*, requires the student to elaborate on his own previous answer—to reconsider it, to modify it, to follow up on it. This kind of question is easy to recognize because it must be addressed to the same pupil that answered the question that immediately preceded it. *Elaborating 2* questions, ones in which one pupil is asked to comment on or react to an answer just made by a different pupil, are not quite so easy to recognize. In order to be classified as *elaborating 2*, a question must be phrased in such a way that the pupil to whom it is directed will not be able to answer it correctly unless he has heard and understood the answer made by some other pupil to the preceding question. This is the kind of question that distinguishes classes in which pupils listen to each other from those in which the interaction consists of a series of dialogues between the teacher and one or another student.

Rhetorical questions, questions raised by the teacher which no one is expected to answer (at least not yet), had already been put in a different category. The name we assigned to this category was borrowed from Withall: *problem structuring*.

One of the limitations imposed by sheer necessity on the new system was that it had to be based entirely on what the teacher said. The audio quality of most of our 50 kineoscopes was so poor that pupil speech was rarely intelligible and therefore inaccessible for coding. We decided to make a virtue of necessity and develop a set of categories based entirely on teacher talk. We saw this as a virtue because it meant that the observer using the system need only pay attention to the teacher: that is, he needed only to observe the behavior of a single person instead of a whole class—a much more circumscribed task.

As a result, we made no attempt at first to distinguish between different types of questions asked by pupils; any event in which a pupil spoke to the teacher except to answer a teacher's question was classified as a *pupil initiation*. Nor did we ask our readers to classify the responses pupils made to teacher questions. Since we knew what kind of question the pupil was asked, the teacher's reaction to the pupil's answer would tell us all we needed to know about the pupil's answer, even when it was inaudible.

The categories we used for coding teacher's reactions to pupil answers (which we called *exits* from *interchanges*) were carried over intact from OScAR 3. There were six of them, two indicating positive feedback, two indicating negative feedback, and two indicating no explicit feedback. Positive feedback indicates that the pupil's answer is correct or acceptable to the teacher; negative feedback indicates that the answer is incorrect or unacceptable. If the exit is neutral in affect, the categories are *approving* (for positive feedback) or *neutrally rejecting* (for negative feedback). If the teacher goes beyond providing feedback and provides either praise (on the positive side) or criticism (on the negative), the exit is coded as *supporting* or *criticizing*.

Our study of the kinescopes verified the fact that teachers often withheld feedback (especially when the pupil's answer was incorrect or unacceptable), and instead merely acknowledged or accepted the pupil's answer by saying something like "un-hum," "I see," or "OK." So when a teacher audibly indicates that she has heard a pupil's answer, without explicity indicating whether it is correct or not, we code the exit as *acknowledging*.

We also noted that in drill sessions in particular, and also when using elaborating questions, teachers sometimes made no overt response to a pupil answer at all, but followed it immediately with another comment. In such a case we classify the exit in a category called *not evaluated*.

By this time we had identified two major types of verbal events in classrooms which we called *teacher statements* and *interchanges*. A *teacher statement* is an event in which the teacher says something to which pupils are supposed to pay attention but not respond. An *interchange* is an event in which a pupil says something which the teacher is expected to evaluate as true or false or as acceptable or unacceptable.

Classroom interaction is highly asymmetrical: the role of the teacher is to evaluate and the role of the pupil is to be evaluated. This is the essential way in which school life differs from real life, in which life as a pupil is different from life anywhere else. In school there is always an evaluator, a person who distinguishes what is true from what is untrue. Perhaps the transition from being a pupil to being a student occurs when the learner no longer depends on an evaluator, a teacher who validates what he learns.

The central event in the classroom, then, is the interchange between pupil and teacher in which some item of substantive content is emitted by the pupil and evaluated by the teacher. Most interchanges are initiated by teacher questions; but some are initiated by pupils. The way in which an interchange begins is called the entry. As we have seen, OScAR 4V recognized four kinds of entries: (1) pupil initiated, (2) convergent, (3) divergent, and (4) elaborating. And we have also seen that it recognized six exits: (1) supporting, (2) approving, (3) acknow-ledge, (4) not evaluated, (5) rejecting, and (6) criticizing. We thus gradually evolved 24 different types of interchanges that could be recognized in a record made with OScAR 4V.

The process by which we developed categories for coding non-substantive interactions and teacher statements was similar to that by which we evolved the categories for coding substantive interchanges. We will not describe them here. Nor will we detail the procedures by which we added the additional categories which led to the replacement of OScAR 4V (which yielded frequencies of 42 types of events) by OScAR 5V (which yields frequencies of 75 types of events). The 18 categories presently used by coders recording behavior with OScAR 5V are shown (with brief definitions) in Figures 5.7 and 5.8.

Each classroom event is identified by a two-digit number, one for the first "word" and one for the second "word." For teacher statements the first digit is a zero and the second is 1 to 9, reflecting the fact that teacher statements are coded in the second word. A teacher statement which communicates content ("Remember that there are four syllables in the word 'evaluate.'") is called informing and represented by 03. The zero identifies it as a *statement*; the 3 as an *informing statement.*

An interchange never begins with zero, because the entry is coded in the first word; a *convergent interchange*, for instance, will have a 6 in the first word. The exit is coded in the second word: a *convergent* question to which a pupil makes an answer that is *approved* is recorded as a 63. Note that two teacher utterances must be coded in order to record this event, one in each word.

A zero is recorded in the second word whenever there is no exit from a teacher initiated interchange—that is, when the pupil does not answer. Thus a problem-structuring statement—a teacher question nobody is supposed to answer, and nobody does answer—is recorded as 50.

By convention, when a pupil speaks to another pupil and the teacher remains silent, the second word is left blank. Thus if one pupil asks a substantive question of another, the event is recorded as 20. If the second pupil responds, that is a new event recorded as 40. Events like these represent a third major category of event, called a *pupil statement*, to add to the two recognized in OScAR 4V, the teacher statement and the interchange.

We have devoted some space to this account of where we began, how we proceeded, and where we ended up in the hope that it will convey some impression to the reader of what a long and difficult process developing a category system can become. The simplicity of the definitions finally adopted is deceptive: it should be emphasized that the simpler the definition, the longer it takes to arrive at it. To develop a set

Symbol	Name	Brief Description
1. PNS	Pupil Utterance Nonsubstantive	Pupil makes a statement or asks a question not related to substance
2. PQU	Pupil Question Substantive	Pupil asks for substantive information
3. PST	Pupil Statement Substantive	Pupil offers substantive information
4. PRS	Pupil Response	Pupil responds directly to another pupil or indirectly to teacher
5. PBST	Problem-Structuring Statement	Teacher raises a substantive question or sets a problem (without indicating who is to answer it)
6. CVG	Convergent Question	Teacher asks pupil a question which calls for one right answer
7. EL1	Elaborating 1 Question	Teacher directs question to the same pupil who answered the question preceding it
8. EL2	Elaborating 2 Question	Teacher directs question to pupil whose answer depends on the preceding one
9. DVG	Divergent Question	Teacher asks pupil a question to which more than one answer may be acceptable or correct

FIGURE 5.7   Behaviors recorded in the first word on OScAR 5V.

of categories that observers can learn to discriminate with a minimum amount of training and can still discriminate accurately some months later takes time. The 18 categories shown in Figures 5.7 and 5.8 are the end product of 10 years of development; and they have survived another 10 years of use, without any need for revision. In a recent study, two coders who received fewer than 10 hours of training established a coefficient of observer agreement of .88 before beginning the study; by the end, after recording behaviors in 36 sessions, this coefficient had increased to .91 (Borich, Malitz, and Kugle, 1978).

There are in existence a small number of well-tested category systems. Ones we know well include Flanders Interaction Analysis

Symbol	Name	Brief Description
1. NOEV	No Evaluation	Teacher does not reply to pupil utterance
2. CNSUP	Considering-Supporting	Teacher utterance with positive affect
3. INFAP	Informing-Approving	Teacher gives information or positive feedback
4. DSCAC	Describing-Accepting	Teacher accepts pupil response or makes statement not otherwise classifiable
5. DIREJ	Directing-Rejecting	Teacher commands pupil to do something or gives negative feedback
6. RBCRT	Rebuking-Criticizing	Teacher utterance with negative affect
7. DST	Desisting	Teacher commands pupil to stop doing something or refuses permission
8. PRNS	Procedural, Neutral-Nonsubstantive Question	Teacher asks question not otherwise classifiable; teacher neither refuses nor gives permission
9. PR+	Procedural, Positive	Teacher offers pupil choice of action or gives permission

FIGURE 5.8   Behaviors recorded in the second word on OScAR 5V.

(Flanders, 1970), Coping Analysis Schedule for Educational Settings (Spaulding, 1982), and the Dyadic Interaction System (Brophy and Good, 1962). Systems such as these have had their reliabilities established over and over again and have been found to yield valid information for a number of different purposes. Anyone considering the use of a category system for routine evaluation of teaching should give careful consideration to adopting one of these instruments before attempting to develop a new one. Remember that the reasons for using a structured observation system are to obtain records of behavior which (1) are accurate and objective, (2) are readily quantifiable without loss of objectivity, and (3) contain behavior data that are relevant to the dimensions of teaching that are to be evaluated.

Any of these four systems can be expected to fulfil the first two requirements far better than any homemade category system could; whether or not it fulfills the third can only be determined by a careful study of the categories it provides for interpretation and scoring—not those the coder uses, which in most cases are different. If these categories reflect aspects of behavior relevant to what you want to assess, we advise you to adopt the system and develop your own scoring keys for it. You will save a great deal of time, effort, and money, and your chances of obtaining valid and reliable evaluations will be much greater than they would be if you tried to build your own system from scratch, or tried to redefine the categories on an existing system.

Our recommendation is the same with regard to multiple coding systems, except that good ones are even more rare than high-quality category systems. The only well-tested ones we are familiar with are PROSE (already described) and the one developed by Stallings and others at the Stanford Research Institute (Stallings, 1977).

Developing a Sign System

There are two sign systems that we can recommend for your consideration. One is CCS, already described. The other is newer, and therefore less highly refined than the ones already mentioned, but has proven useful in a variety of applications in its relatively short life. It is called COKER (Classroom Observations Keyed for Effectiveness Research), and is unique in that it was designed for evaluation rather than research. Specifically, it was designed to provide coverage of as many aspects of classroom behavior as possible, and to include only behavior items which primia facia evidence indicated to be related to teacher effectiveness. Considerable evidence has been accumulated to show that COKER yields useful and reliable data (Coker and Coker, 1979a, b).

A sign system is the easiest kind of system to construct, to refine, and to use. To develop one as sophisticated as CCS takes about as much testing, revision, and retesting, as it would to develop a category system. But less sophisticated sign systems can be very useful. Before you attempt to build an entirely new system we recommend that you consider using one of the two mentioned. COKER, in particular, is almost sure to contain tested items related to any dimension you are likely to need. It makes sense to take advantage of the considerable head start it could provide by beginning with it.

If you feel that you must develop a new system and are willing to commit the necessary resources to the project you must still begin by listing the specific behaviors that need to be recorded to provide a basis for the evaluations you wish to make. Once this is done, check again to make certain that no existing instrumentation provides the information you need. Then solicit the help of someone who has had experience in constructing such systems. Such help will be most useful in the next step, which is that of converting your list of behaviors to a set of observable items or signs.

Years ago some suggestions were offered about how to write sign items that could be recorded objectively (Medley and Mitzel, 1963). One critical point made was that a sign should refer to a *single event: Teacher asks a convergent question,* not *Teacher asks convergent questions* or *Teacher asks many convergent questions.* It is easy for the recorder to recognize when an event occurs once. What is difficult is to keep some sort of a running count while observing other behaviors; what is risky is to try to remember how many there were at the end of a period. The single-event item is almost certain to be more reliable then either of the other two.

There are two types of signs: *dynamic* and *static*. The example above is dynamic: it refers to an event that occurs at a certain moment in time and is over. A static sign refers, not to an event, but to a condition that persists for some time. *Teacher central* is a *static* sign; it refers to a continuing condition rather than to a event. Static signs are best recorded at the end of the period; dynamic signs are best recorded on occurrence, although in practice there will often be some dynamic signs that have been observed during the period but not yet recorded when the period ends.

It is important that a sign be easy to recognize when it is observed; that is, that the cue or cues, or the basis of which it is to be recognized, be overt and explicit. Above all, it is important that a sign be recognizable by the recorder with minimal need to draw inferences about unobservable cognitive processes, intentions, and the like. If inferences must be made, they should be ones that the teachers' pupils must make.

Frequent tryouts and revisions are important in which several observers record the same performances, and between tryouts discuss reasons for disagreements in their records, and (if necessary) redefine the signs involved.

Events or conditions that are conspicuous or that occur relatively infrequently make better signs than ones that are more common and less conspicuous. *Pupil cries* is likely to be a more reliable item than *pupil smiles,* even though both seem to share a common factor. This is so because (in most classes) pupils smile more often than they cry, and because smiles are harder to spot then tears.

Traditionally, the constructor of a new sign system borrows items freely from earlier systems. Even OScAR 2a, one of the earliest to appear (Medley and Mitzel, 1958) drew heavily on an earlier system, an instrument used by Cornell, Lindvall, and Saupe (1952). CCS, in turn, began life as a strengthened version of OScAR 2a. The items on COKER were adapted from five category and sign systems: FLACCS (Soar, Soar, and Ragosta, 1971), OScAR 5V, STARS (Spaulding, 1970), CASES

(Spaulding, 1969), and TPOR (Brown, 1970) and were selected because they were found to be the most reliable and valid in predicting student outcomes. As has been noted, it is relatively easy to add items to or delete items from a sign system at any point in its development or its actual use. Such changes need not affect scoring keys already in use, but should strongly affect future keys.

SUMMARY

In this chapter we have discussed three major types of structured observation systems: category systems, sign systems, and multiple coding systems; and have presented examples of each in some detail. We have also briefly discussed some points related to the construction of category and sign systems. We have advised the reader to undertake the considerable task of developing a new system only if it is absolutely necessary; that is, if no existing system or systems can be adapted to his purpose. We have also suggested that the reader who decides to build his own system should build a sign system rather than either a category or multiple coding system because a sign system is much easier to build and to revise than either of the other two.

BIBLIOGRAPHY

Ashton, P. T., R. B. Webb, and N. Dodl. *A Study of Teachers' Sense of Efficacy.* Gainseville: University of Florida, 1983. (N. I. E. Contract no. 1-40-79-0075).

Bloom, B. S., M. D. Engelhart, E. J. Furst, W. H. Hill, and D. R. Krathwohl, eds. *Taxonomy of Educational Objectives: The Classification of Educational Goals, Handbook I: Cognitive Domain.* New York: David McKay, 1956.

Borich, G. D., D. Malitz, and C. L. Kugle. "Convergent and Discriminant Validity of Five Classroom Observation Schedules: Testing a Model." *Journal of Educational Psychology,* 1978, *70,* 119–128.

Brophy, J., and T. Good. *Teacher Child Dyadic Interaction: A Manual for Coding Classroom Behavior.* Research and Development Center for Teacher Education, Austin, TX: 1962, publ. no. 0043.

Brown, B. B. "Experimentalism in Teaching Practice." *Journal of Research and Development in Education,* 1970, *4,* 14–22.

Coker, Homer, and Joan G. Coker. *Classroom Observations Keyed for Effectiveness Research—Observer Training Manual.* Atlanta, GA: Georgia State University/Carroll County Teacher Corps Project, 1979 (a).

——— *Classroom Observations Keyed for Effectiveness Research—User's Manual.* Atlanta, GA: Georgia State University/Carroll County Teacher Corps Project, 1979 (b).

Cornell, F. G., C. M. Lindvall, and J. L. Saupe. *An Exploratory Measurement of*

Individualities of Schools and Classrooms. Bureau of Educational Research, College of Education, University of Illinois, September, 1952.

Flanders, N. A. *Analyzing Teaching Behavior.* Reading, MA: Addison-Wesley, 1970.

Holt, John. *How Children Fail.* New York, Pitman, 1967.

Medley, Donald M. "The Language of Teacher Behavior: Communicating the Results of Structured Observations to Teachers." *Journal of Teacher Education,* 1971, *22,* 157–165.

Medley, Donald M., and Harold E. Mitzel. "A Technique for Measuring Classroom Behavior." *Journal of Educational Psychology,* 1958, *49,* 86–92.

———— "Development of the Observation Schedules." In H. Schueler, M. J. Gold, and H. E. Mitzel, eds., *The Use of Television for Improving Teacher Training and for Improving Measures of Student-Teaching Performance. Phase I: Improvement of Student Teaching* New York: Hunter College, 1962.

———— "Measuring Classroom Behavior by Systematic Observation." In N. L. Gage, ed. *Handbook of Research on Teaching.* Chicago, IL: Rand McNally, 1963.

Soar, Robert S., and Ruth M. Soar. *Climate and Control System.* Gainesville, FL: College of Education, University of Florida, 1982 (a).

———— "Observing the Classroom." In D. E. Orlosky, ed, *Introduction to Education.* Columbus, OH: Merrill, 1982 (b).

Soar, R. S., R. M. Soar, and M. Ragosta. *Florida Climate and Control System (FLACCS): Observer's Manual.* Gainesville, FL: Institute for the Department of Human Resources, University of Florida, 1971.

Spaulding, Robert L. *Classroom Behavior Analysis and Treatment.* Durham, NC: Education Improvement Program, Duke University, 1969.

———— *Spaulding Teacher Activity Recording Schedule (STARS).* San Jose, CA: San Jose State University, 1970.

Spaulding, Robert L., and C. L. Spaulding. *Research-Based Classroom Management.* Los Gatos, CA: 1982.

Stallings, J. A. *Learning to Look: A Handbook on Classroom Observation and Teaching Models.* Belmont, CA: Wadsworth, 1977.

Withall, J. "The Development of a Technique for the Measurement of Social-Emotional Climate in Classrooms." *Journal of Experimental Education,* 1949, *17,* 347–361.

Defining the Task to Be Performed

You should remember from Chapter 2 that the second step in the process of evaluating human performance, defining the task to be performed, is important for three reasons.

1. To elicit a sample of relevant teacher behaviors, one on which a valid evaluation can be based.
2. To ensure that the tasks assigned to teachers whose performances are to be compared are comparable in difficulty.
3. To provide a basis for scoring the record of performance—i.e., to make it possible to discriminate appropriate behaviors from inappropriate ones.

In this chapter we will discuss this problem of defining the task as it applies to the evaluation of teaching performance and of teacher competence.

Very little formal attention has been paid to this problem in the past, and there is very little empirical knowledge about it; but if we want to evaluate either performance or competence objectively and validly we must deal with the problem as best we can. What we have to offer you consists mainly of suggestions which are largely untested. Before we do that there are some preliminary matters we should discuss briefly.

We should remind ourselves, for one thing, about the difference between evaluating what a teacher *does* in a given situation—what we call *performance*—and evaluating what a teacher *is*, what she is able to do or may be expected to do in other situations—what we call *competence*. Equally competent teachers, like equally skilled athletes, may perform quite differently in a given setting. The race does not always go to the swift; if it did, horse races would be dull affairs and teacher evaluation would be much easier than it is.

When we observe a teacher with a class we can obtain an accurate, objective record of her performance by following the procedures described in this book. But we cannot develop valid measurements either of how well she has performed or of how competent she is except in terms of the task she was trying to carry out. It is necessary, then, either to set a task for the teacher to perform or to let the teacher decide what she is trying to do and arrive at a clear understanding of it. Either approach will give us a critical element in the definition of the task that we need before we can assign scoring weights to the events in the record. Only if we know what the teacher's purpose is can we assign positive weights to relevant behaviors that reflect best practice for accomplishing the teacher's purpose, zero weights to ones that are irrelevant, and negative weights to relevant behaviors that do not correspond to best practice.

In order to make the tasks performed by different teachers comparable, we must also concern ourselves with factors that affect teacher performance that are not under her control, with what we have identified in Figure 2.1 as contextual factors. We are concerned primarily with Type I or *external context*, with such obvious things as the grade or subject the teacher teaches, and the physical, cultural, and socio-economic environment in which she teaches, and with others not quite so obvious. We must also concern ourselves with Type II or *internal context*, with such things as the average level of pupils' ability, previous achievement, self-concept, attitude toward school, the amount of variability on each of these, and the makeup of the class as regards sex and ethnic origin of pupils and number (and types) of mainstreamed pupils. These factors directly affect pupil behavior and indirectly affect teacher behavior. Finally, the nature of the task defined—the purpose that the teacher is trying to achieve—must be such that any teacher competent and motivated to perform the task may be expected to perform it.

There is a basic human right involved in any kind of assessment which is often overlooked when teachers are being assessed: the teacher's right to do her best when she is being evaluated. It is accepted without question that in order for a pupil's score on any aptitude or achievement test to be valid, the pupil must do his best—must mark the right answer to any item if he can figure out what it is. Unless he does this, the pupil's test score will not be a valid measure of his aptitude or achievement.

This, by the way, is a major reason why so many questionnaires designed to measure attitudes, interests, values, and the like lack validity. If the person answering the questionnaire perceives it as a test (as is likely when it is administered as part of a selection procedure) he will be motivated to do his best to mark the "correct" response to each item. When, for instance, the alternative responses to an item like "How often do you have headaches?" include one choice (such as *often*), which happens to be true, and one (such as *rarely*), which seems more likely to be keyed as correct, the highly motivated person will often mark the latter.

Early, less sophisticated attitude inventories depended for their validity on the assumption that the candidate would choose the *true* response rather than the one he or she perceives as correct; as a result they tended to have little validity. Later, more sophisticated instruments do not depend on this assumption; instead, they are designed to correct for the tendency of candidates to respond to the inventory as though it were a test.

When a teacher's performance is being evaluated, it is just as important to the validity of the evaluation that the teacher be motivated to do her best as it is when she takes any other kind of a test. We must measure what a teacher can do in the classroom in the same way we measure what she knows, on the basis of her ability to recognize "correct" responses to relevant problems. A notion has grown up that we should judge teachers on the basis of what they do when they are not being evaluated. This not only does not make sense; it also violates the teacher's basic human right to put her best foot forward; at the same time it destroys the validity of the evaluation.

This point is germaine to the problem of task definition. It is common practice for the rater to say to a teacher: "I am here to evaluate you; please go on with whatever you were doing just as though I were not here." This is not only unrealistic; it threatens the teacher's right to do her best. Fortunately for the validity of the ratings (which need all the validity they can get) most teachers ignore this threat and do the best they can, anyhow. A more enlightened practice some administrators use is to ask the teacher to invite the evaluator in some time when she is at her best.

One problem with this is that the teacher's perception of her best performance may be very different from the rater's idea of what good teaching is; we would have a teacher demonstrating one competency and being evaluated on another. From this we can see the importance of a clear task definition—one in which what the teacher is trying to do is perceived in the same way by the teacher and the evaluator. Only such a definition can elicit a competent performance from a competent teacher, and at the same time ensure that appropriate scoring weights can be assigned to behaviors that she exhibits.

Current practice in teacher evaluation succeeds by effectively ignoring the problem; when a supervisor or administrator observes and rates a teacher performance as a basis for evaluating the teacher, any mutual understanding of what the teacher is supposed to do is implicit. The assumption seems to be that the supervisor and the teacher both know what good teaching is, what behaviors are appropriate or inappropriate under the circumstances prevailing when the observation is made. This is about as vague a definition of the teacher's task as one can imagine. Any dissonance that may exist between the teacher's concept of what the rater is looking for and what he is actually looking for operates as error of measurement and lessens both the reliability of the evaluation and, as a result, its validity. Anything that we can do to reduce such dissonance, to clarify the definition of the task the teacher is to perform, will certainly increase the reliability and almost certainly increase the validity of the measurements. It is by no means necessary to achieve a perfect definition in order to improve reliability and validity substantially, however. It is our contention that we can do a far better job than we are doing now by taking some steps; and that what we can achieve is limited chiefly by the amount of effort we are willing to make.

LEVELS OF TEACHER COMPETENCE

Before we get specific about how to go about this, we need to define the levels of teacher competence at which we propose to work. Figure 6.1 shows in yet another flow chart three levels of teacher competence at which objectives of teacher training have been defined. We find that it is useful to view them as hierarchically related.

The lowest level is that of *teaching skill*: a teacher functioning at this level is competent to execute a lesson plan; that is, to go into a classroom and see that the pupils in it have the experiences or engage in the activities specified in a lesson plan. Teaching skill can be evaluated, if the nature of the plan is known, by comparing what happens with what is supposed to happen. The lesson plan will specify how the teacher is to behave (strategy) and how the pupils are to behave (objectives); these are the behaviors to be observed and recorded; which are appropriate or inappropriate is specified by the plan.

The second level of teacher competence is the ability to develop a lesson plan (or instructional strategy) which, if implemented, will result in optimal learning outcomes—in maximum progress toward the objectives set for the class the teacher teaches. Given such a set of objectives the teacher who has achieved competence in *instructional design* can design instruction which, if carried out, will achieve these objectives. If the plan conforms to best practice the teacher has performed competently.

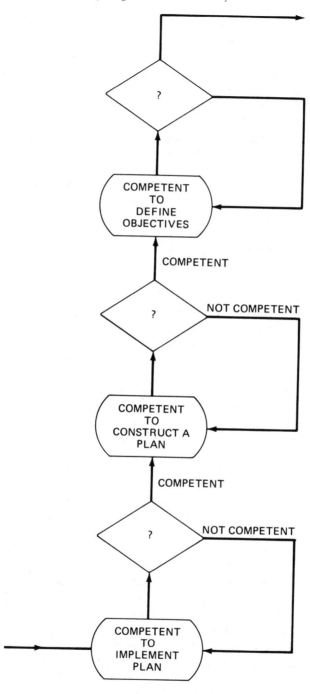

FIGURE 6.1   Levels of teacher competence.

The third level of teacher competence has to do with *defining objectives*. Given a particular class of pupils and a set of goals set for this school in this community, the competent teacher can define a set of objectives appropriate to the class and the goals which if achieved will maximize the progress of the class toward the goals. Once again, the set of objectives will conform to best practice.

This book deals only with the evaluation of teaching skill; that is, with the lowest of these three levels of competency. It seems to us that teaching skill is the key to successful operation of the entire educational enterprise; without competent teaching the enterprise cannot succeed. Statements of objectives and plans for achieving them are worthless unless they can be and are executed in the classroom.

At present the amount of sound knowledge we have about any one of these three levels of competence is slight, far below the minimum we need; but we cannot even test the validity of hypotheses about defining objectives or designing instruction until we can implement these designs in the classroom. We desperately need knowledge both of human learning on which to base instructional designs and of the nature of teaching skill so that we can identify and develop ways of teaching it.

It is difficult at this point to predict how the schools of the future will assign the roles defined by the three levels of competence. There are proposals for staff differentiation which would have some teachers responsible only for implementing instruction, others (with higher status) responsible for designing it, with objectives being defined at an even higher level. It is not too long since we heard a great deal about teacher-proof materials, materials that relieved teachers of need for the higher levels of competence. There is no way of predicting exactly what the schools of the future will be like; but it is safe to say that at the point of contact between the school system and the pupil there will be a teacher responsible for carrying out some kind of plan who will need teaching skill.

In Figure 4.2 we analyzed teaching skill into three component parts: environmental maintenance, implementation of the lesson plan, and maintenance of pupil involvement. From the standpoint of teacher evaluators, these may also be seen as hierarchically related, with environmental maintenance at the lowest or simplest level, and maintenance of pupil involvement at the highest or most complex. Skill in maintaining the learning environment is the simplest of these to measure, mainly because it does not vary as much with the nature of the plan the teacher is trying to implement as the others do. Experience in process-product research clearly shows that this aspect of teaching skill can be measured objectively, reliably, and validly from records made without regard to what plan the teacher is following (or to most other contextual factors). The researchers make their observations at times chosen haphazardly (if not randomly), and find that this aspect of teacher performance is stable across such observations. Teachers seem to create and maintain a classroom environment that does not change appreciably as the type of lesson varies.

We therefore suggest that any effort you make to implement measurement-based teacher evaluation should begin at this level: you should start out by focusing on teachers' skill in establishing and maintaining a classroom environment favorable to learning. We have already described and exemplified some of the dimensions of classroom environment in Chapter 4. You may prefer to define it differently; but in our discussion we shall assume that it includes but is not limited to what is generally called classroom management. This term seems to be a euphemism for maintaining order in the classroom; maintaining order is an element, and an important one, in environmental maintenance. But a favorable learning environment must also have an affective or emotional tone and an intellectual or cognitive one that foster learning. Or so we shall assume.

Once a system for assessing and developing teachers' skill in this area is in operation, we expect—or hope—that most of you will want to take the next step to assess instructional skill; that is, the ability to implement a predefined teaching strategy or lesson plan. This is more difficult, but we believe that when it is to become part of an evaluation system already in place, it can be done. (See, for example, Spaulding and Spaulding, 1983.)

ASSESSING SKILL IN ENVIRONMENTAL MAINTENANCE

When we speak of a system for assessing and developing skill in environmental maintenance we envisage something more than a system for evaluating teachers. It is a system based on an objective evaluation system, but it also includes mechanisms for providing help to teachers who need it in improving their skill. There is a consensus between teachers and supervisory staff about the kind of learning environment that is to exist in the school or school system. There is instrumentation which can be used to obtain an accurate, objective diagnostic description of the environment in a classroom and to detect changes over time, and a mechanism for helping teachers improve.

The existence of a consensus about the nature of the desired learning environment provides a definition of the task the teacher is to perform whenever she is evaluated which is clearly understood by all concerned. In particular, there is a basis for developing scoring keys for observation records that will yield valid measurements on the various dimensions included in the definition. Each teacher will know what is expected of her and how to behave in order to earn the best score possible at her own level of skill; nobody will be trying to display irrelevant or inappropriate behaviors. The evaluation will be fair. Evaluations of performance—of how well the teacher does with the class and under existing conditions—will be as accurate and as valid as the quality of the instrumentation and the available resources permit. Evaluations of competence—of how well the teacher can perform—will require some steps to equate the difficulties of tasks that different teachers do perform, however. We have two strategies to suggest.

The first strategy is one we shall call a *nonintervention* strategy, because it uses existing intact classes. Comparability of classes is achieved to a degree by attempting to compensate for important differences by statistical adjustments made in the records as part of the scoring process.

Use of this strategy depends on obtaining and using information about contextual factors, both internal and external. Such things as grade and subject, school (if the evaluation systems operates in more than one), and certain test score data would be important.

For illustrative purposes, let us say that we are working in the elementary schools in a district which has a sizeable non-English-speaking minority unevenly distributed among its school buildings; that the testing program periodically provides scores of all pupils on an achievement battery; and that indices of socioeconomic and marital status of parents are also available.

Each record of teacher performance should also contain the following information: grade level, school building, proportion of minority pupils in the class, and the mean and standard deviation of scores of the pupils in the class on the most recent preceding administration of the school testing program for each subtest in the battery.

As soon as the first complete set of data obtained in all of the elementary schools in the district becomes available, equations will be set up for adjusting the frequency of each item of behavior in a record to compensate for differences on these contextual factors. In the future this adjustment would be incorporated into the computer program for scoring the records.

The effect of this would be to weight each behavior item according to how appropriate the behavior is in a class in that grade and school, with the same characteristics (minority-group members, SES, and mean and range of achievement) as the class the teacher taught during the observation.

The principal weakness in this strategy lies in the possibility that there may be a major contextual factor of whose existence—or importance—we are unaware and which we overlook, a factor that destroys or greatly reduces the validity of our measurements.

This does not seem to us to be likely enough to give us much worry, but the only way we can be certain that such a thing does not happen is to use the second alternative strategy described below. On the positive side, the preliminary regression analysis may identify contextual factors that strongly affect teacher performance about which something can be done. It may be possible by some minor change in policy which makes the teacher's task easier to produce a dramatic improvement in her performance.

Our second strategy is an *interventionist* strategy; it involves manipulation of pupil assignments to classes. Specifically, it requires the introduction of restricted random assignment of pupils to classes.

One set of restrictions is imposed by the school and grade (or subject) that the pupil is in. One obviously cannot assign pupils to grades or subjects at random; or to the school districts or school buildings within a district. We must therefore divide our population of pupils into groups within which random assignment is possible.

This process ensures that all classes will be closely similar in all respects, not only in those factors that are identified but in others of which we may be unaware. The difficulties of the tasks different teachers must perform will not be identical, but they will be as nearly so as is humanly possible; and it will be possible to assess the differences in difficulties with considerable precision and take account of them in interpreting the scores obtained. Within these limits, any differences in performances of different teachers may safely be attributed to differences in the competence of teachers within the group.

This kind of randomization is by far the fairest possible to both teachers and pupils. If school policy required segregation of certain kinds of pupils in special classes—exceptional children, perhaps—we would certainly not evaluate the teachers of such a special class in the same way that we evaluated teachers of randomly constituted classes. This procedure would justify comparisons only between teachers within the same school and grade, or other randomization group. That is, norms could not be set up for any larger group.

In order to permit comparisons between teachers in different schools or of different grades and subjects, we must adjust frequencies in the behavior records on grade, subject, and school in the same way we would make adjustments on these and other contextual factors if we were following the first strategy.

This may all sound very complicated. In actuality, the description is a good deal more complex than the operation; in these days of high-speed computers and microprocessors, the complexities may be dealt with once and for all when the computer programs are written; operation is a routine affair. The programming task is not difficult as such things go: what looks to us like a can of worms is duck soup to a programmer (metaphorically speaking).

Remember that what we are trying to do is to assess directly some of the most complex and poorly understood phenomena known to science; it would be naive indeed to expect that any process by which this can be accomplished should be simple or easy. It is largely because we have grossly underestimated the complexity of the problem in the past, so much so that we have assumed that any busy school administrator could do it on the basis of impressions formed during a casual visit or two to a teacher's class, that the quality of instruction in the schools has shown so little improvement for many decades.

If it is important to you to have dependable information about the strengths and weaknesses of teachers for any purpose, you must be prepared to go to whatever trouble it takes to obtain such data. The approach we are presenting is, we believe, perfectly feasible and, though by no means easy or inexpensive, the least difficult (and most economical) one available.

The step with which we have been concerned in this chapter, that of arriving at a definition of the task a teacher is to perform when she is evaluated, is critically important and has been almost completely ignored in the past. So long as you limit your goal to evaluating teachers' skill in maintaining the learning environment, defining the task is relatively simple. But sooner or later you will have to deal with the more difficult task of measuring and improving instructional skill, which is the heart of teaching.

MEASURING INSTRUCTIONAL SKILL

By this time you should have some insight into our reason for recommending that you begin to implement measurement-based teacher evaluation by concentrating on the simplest element to evaluate. Only after you have gone through the process, and your teachers and supervisors have found out that the approach works, should you attempt to apply it to instructional skill, where defining the task is so much more complex.

Most other phases of your evaluation program will remain unchanged as you move into this second phase. If you have chosen your instrument well you can continue to use it, and continue to include in the records the same data about contextual factors. The principal operational changes will result from the need for a more detailed definition of the task which will specify more clearly the lesson plan or instructional strategy the teacher is trying to implement than has been necessary up to this point.

There are two alternative strategies for defining instructional tasks: one is inductive, one deductive. The difference between the two has to do with how you arrive at a definition of skillful or competent implementation of a plan or strategy. Consensus about skillful instruction is more difficult to achieve than consensus about what constitutes an environment favorable to learning. The research has little to tell us about it; theoreticians do not agree, nor do custodians of the lore of the profession. There is little agreement on what the various strategies which call for different patterns of implementations are, much less on how any of them should be implemented.

What we shall call a *deductive* approach involves selecting a single strategy or type of lesson, defining a way of implementing it which will be considered correct in your setting, and adopting as the staff development goal learning to implement the strategy in this way. What we shall call an *inductive* approach involves developing a system for classifying lesson plans into categories, the successful implementation of each of which calls for a different pattern of teacher behavior (which may or may not be known). Performances of all teachers in the school system are observed, recorded, and analyzed to ascertain how the most effective teachers implement each type of plan.

If your major concern is with being able to evaluate teachers' overall instructional skill, you will probably do best by following the inductive strategy, which involves undertaking some of the research necessary to support the kind of evaluation program you need yourself. But if you are at least as much interested in improving instruction as you are in evaluating it, the simpler deductive strategy may be best for you. We shall discuss this approach next.

A Deductive Approach to the Evaluation of Instructional Skill

Let us assume that you have already put into effect a measurement-based evaluation and staff development system designed to improve teachers' skill in environmental maintenance, and it has succeeded well enough so that you are looking for new worlds to conquer. The first thing that you should do is to identify a type of lesson plan or a teaching strategy that is important to most or all of your teachers and can be clearly defined. A particular way of teaching concepts, such as one can find in Joyce and Weil's *Models of Teaching* (1980) might be an example. Acquiring skill in implementing this model might be adopted as an objective to be achieved by all teachers during a particular semester.

The next step is to define successful implementation of the strategy in operational terms—that is, to develop a key for scoring a performance record to indicate how closely the behavior recorded corresponds to that strategy. If records made with the instrument you have been using can be scored to measure implementations of the strategy, so much the better. If not, you will have to repeat the process described in Chapter 4 and either select a new instrument or construct one and retrain your observers.

You are now ready to evaluate teachers' skill in this particular type of instruction. The task the teacher is to perform each time she is evaluated must be defined in such a way that her performance will yield a valid measure of this particular skill. This means that the plan the teacher tries to implement must be one which calls for this strategy; in our example, the plan must call for the kind of behavior specified in the model. If the teacher should happen to be teaching something else besides concepts, or if she should have planned to teach concepts in some other way, a valid assessment will not be obtained.

The evaluation may be scheduled at a time when the teacher intends to use the strategy; or the teacher may arrange her schedule so that she will be using it when the observer visits her class. Contextual data should be incorporated in the record just as they are when skill in environmental maintenance is being assessed. The procedure already described should be used to adjust the frequencies of individual behavior items as part of the scoring process. Thus the purposes of task definition are all fulfilled: the sample of behavior is relevant, there is a basis for scoring the record, and the tasks faced by different teachers are comparable.

As the process of staff development goes on, making full use of the diagnostic information in the performance records, periodic reevaluations will be made to assess each teacher's rate of progress.

In succeeding semesters or years, skills in implementing other plans or strategies can be fostered in the same way.

An Inductive Approach to the Evaluation of Instructional Skill

As has been noted, this approach is not as well adapted to a program in which staff development goals are predefined. Instead, each teacher defines for herself the plan or strategy she wishes to learn to implement successfully; that is, she defines her own goal. When an observer visits a teacher to record her performance it is understood that the plan or strategy that the teacher will try to implement during the visit will be chosen by the teacher. It may be the same one she would have tried to implement at that time if she were not being evaluated; it may be one she would not otherwise attempt because she is having difficulty with it and would like help in implementing it. Records made when this approach is used must contain, in addition to the information about external and internal context, detailed information about the teacher's plan obtained in an interview with the teacher *before* the performance is recorded.

Multiple scoring keys must be developed, one for each type of plan or instructional category in a set of types of plans so constructed that implementation of all plans in any one category call for similar patterns of teacher behavior. Thus (in effect) the evaluation of the performance is based on the degree to which the performance conforms to what that teacher herself is trying to do. As soon as enough data become available a series of regression analyses should be done for each type, each of which has the frequency of one item of behavior as the dependent variable and includes as independent variables not only external and internal contextual factors but also relevant data about the teacher's plan. From these analyses formulas for adjusting behavior frequencies can be developed and applied to the scores on each record.

We shall not go into any more detail about the inductive approach here. It represents the most sophisticated and difficult level of application of measurement-based teacher evaluation that we will mention in this volume. No one is likely to reach this level for some years, and not until having acquired a good deal of experience in defining evaluation tasks at the two simpler levels.

SUMMARY

This chapter has dealt with the problem of arriving at an understanding between the evaluator and the teacher being evaluated of the nature of the task the teacher is to perform while her behavior is being recorded for later evaluation. Such an understanding is what is meant by a task definition.

A clear task definition is necessary first, to ensure that the record contains relevant behaviors; second, to ensure that records of different performances will be comparable; and third, to make it possible to discriminate appropriate from inappropriate behaviors so that the record can be scored.

Just what is involved in the definition of a task depends on the type of competencies that are to be evaluated. Our concern in this volume is limited to competencies displayed in the classroom while the teacher is interacting with her pupils. Among these, we propose to evaluate (1) those relevant to creating and maintaining a classroom environment favorable to learning, and (2) those relevant to the implementation of a plan or strategy previously specified (see Figure 4.2). Our recommendation is that measurement-based teacher evaluation should not be applied to competencies at the second level until it has been successfully used to evaluate competencies on the first.

A task definition must specify three aspects of the task: (1) the nature of the plan or strategy the teacher is trying to carry out, (2) the external context, and (3) the internal context (see Figure 2.1). When skill in maintaining the environment is being evaluated, the first of these three dimensions can be disregarded; otherwise all three are relevant.

Relevance of the behavior in a record and the basis for scoring it are both assured by the fact that maintaining the environment is a task the teacher faces whenever she teaches. Comparability is achieved either by direct intervention or by statistical adjustment. Interventions may include manipulation of pupil assignments to control internal context; these are discussed in some detail. Where intervention is impractical or undesirable, context factors must be measured and item frequencies must be adjusted to compensate for differences in these factors. This is done as part of the scoring process.

Assessment of instructional skill requires, in addition, that the task definition be quite explicit about the plan or strategy that the teacher is following. When the evaluation system is part of a staff development program, acquisition of a particular competency or aspect of instructional skill is adopted as a goal of the program, and records of performance are made only when the plan or strategy involves that competency. This is the simplest way of defining an instructional task and the one we recommend be used in the second stage of implementation of an evaluation system; it is referred to as the deductive approach.

An inductive approach was also discussed briefly—one in which the plan a teacher is to follow is not arranged, but is incorporated in the record, and the scoring key is based on what the teacher defines as appropriate behavior. After a substantial amount of data have been collected they are analyzed to verify that the scoring keys do in fact reflect competent performance for the types of plans for which they were developed.

BIBLIOGRAPHY

Joyce, B., and M. Weil. *Models of Teaching*. 2d ed. Englewood Cliffs, NJ: Prentice-Hall, 1980.

Spaulding, Robert L., and Cheryl L. Spaulding. *Research-Based Classroom Management*. Los Gatos, CA: Author, 1982.

7

Obtaining the Record

The preceding chapters of this book have dealt with procedures for developing or selecting a systematic observation schedule for use in a teacher evaluation system. This chapter will discuss procedures for obtaining valid records with such an instrument, once it has been decided upon. Some of the questions we will attempt to answer are these.

- How do you go about the task of recruiting or selecting the personnel who are to observe classroom behaviors and to obtain the behavior records on which the evaluations are to be based? What kind of person should you look for? Should you use supervisors or others trained in teacher evaluation?
- How many records of behavior must be made in each teacher's class, and how and by whom will the observations be scheduled? How should a classroom observer behave in the school and the classroom?
- How do you test an observation system, and how do you evaluate the results of the test?

Before we attempt to answer these and related questions, we would like to emphasize once more how desirable it is that everyone who will be affected by the teacher evaluation program be involved at every step in the development of the program, from the establishment of its goals to the development of the procedures for using the evaluation data after they are obtained. All procedures used should be as open as sound evaluation will permit; the rationale behind the procedures should be clearly understood and accepted by all; the teachers in particular should have a genuine role in decisions made about what happens to them as a result of the evaluations.

We would like also to note that the recommendations we make in the pages to follow will be based on our collective experience of more than 50 years in the collection and analysis of records made with instruments closely similar to those you will be using, not for use in teacher evaluation but for use in research on classroom teaching. You should bear this in mind in judging how sound the advice is.

Teachers share the natural human tendency to feel anxious when they know they are being evaluated; they are particularly anxious when their classroom behavior is observed for this purpose. No less an authority than the president of the American Federation of Teachers has asserted, however, that teachers do not fear evaluation that is unbiased (Shanker, 1983). What they do fear are subjective approaches that do not provide records or standards that are open and public.

The availability of portable and relatively inexpensive videotape recording equipment may seem to provide a particularly easy and inexpensive way of obtaining complete and objective records of classroom behavior; but, since each and every videotape recording must be viewed and coded by a trained observer before it can be used for teacher evaluation, you cannot really save any money this way. On the contrary, it will cost you quite a bit more to obtain the same amount of data if you use videotape, because you will need to pay for just as much observer time, plus whatever it costs to secure the videotape recordings. Worse yet, the evaluations you end up with are likely to be quite a bit less valid. One reason for this is that it is easier to code live behavior accurately than behavior recorded on tape. Another reason is that the presence in the classroom of a cameraman and camera are more intrusive and more likely to distort the behaviors of both pupils and teachers than the presence of a single human observer. The fact is that observing a classroom on a TV monitor is much more like watching it through a keyhole than actually visiting the classroom.

OBSERVER RECRUITMENT AND SELECTION

Once your evaluation program has been designed, who should be selected and trained to make records of behavior with the instrument or instruments you have chosen?

Smith (1980), speaking in the context of preservice teacher education, makes a point that is equally applicable in the context of in-service teacher education:

> Since objective observation is the *sine qua non* of professional work, it must be considered as a primary domain of pedagogical training. It will need to be attended to throughout the period of professional preparation. (p. 93)

This is confirmed by research which indicates that significant changes in the classroom performance of teachers occur when the teachers themselves are trained to use a low-inference observation system (Amidon and Hough, 1967). This seems to happen because the categories in the observation system provide a new "language" which the teachers can use in thinking about and monitoring their own behavior and in discussing it with supervisors (cf. Medley, 1971).

The supervisor's ability to function effectively in this process depends on his fluency in this language, that is, knowledge of the system. The supervisor or other administrator responsible for improving instruction must therefore acquire a good working knowledge of any observation system he proposes to use for teacher evaluation. Such a working knowledge is available only to someone well enough trained in the system to be competent to function as a trained classroom observer.

This does not mean that the administrator should be expected personally to collect the data that will be used for evaluation purposes. The school administrator has other responsibilities which only he is qualified to discharge; it would be an inefficient use of the administrator's time to have him do something a less highly trained person can do as well. The appropriate role of the administrator in improving instruction involves *interpreting* records made by other personnel rather than collecting them. There is really no more reason for the principal to collect observational data to make decisions about teachers than for him to administer achievement tests to make decisions about pupils.

When you consider who should be trained to observe and record classroom behavior, your primary concern will be with those who will be responsible for making the records on which the evaluations will be based, so it may be useful to consider the role that the classroom observer is expected to play in the evaluation program.

The Role of the Observer

The primary role that the observer must play is that of a process recorder, which is to observe and record the occurrence of the behaviors or categories of behavior specified by the observation system being used. The principal skill that such a recorder must possess, then, is the ability to observe and accurately *code* classroom behaviors—that is, to recognize which of the behaviors that occur during an observation period are to be recorded, and which sign or category each one exemplifies. How skillful the recorder is determines more than anything else how accurate the records are that he makes. How valid a record is depends on its accuracy, on how closely it corresponds to what actually happened. Observers vary in this respect; the degree of accuracy in any given observer's record will be referred to as the *observer validity* of the observer.

In order to fulfill his role the classroom observer must establish and maintain constructive professional relationships with the teachers he observes. In particular, the observer must treat anything that occurs during a classroom visit as privileged information in much the same sense that what passes between a physician and a patient or between an attorney and a client is. The record of behavior must be treated as a confidential document that is not to be discussed with or shown to anyone except through the channels set up as part of the evaluation system.

It should perhaps be reemphasized that evaluating teachers is no part of the recorder's role. The recorder must resist as much as possible the temptation to judge any of the teachers whose behavior he observes, and above all must not reveal any opinions he may form. The observer should have no clear idea of the weights or other scoring numbers that will be attached to any of the items in the record.

Observer Selection

Because the observer's role is restricted to observing and recording, not evaluating teacher performance, it is neither necessary nor desirable to employ highly trained professionals as observers.

When rating scales are used to evaluate teachers, the professional expertise and pedagogical knowledge of the rater are critically important. This is so because both the record of behavior and the standards the rater uses exist only in the mind of the rater, so that the validity of the ratings depends heavily on the quality of the observer's judgment. But when a structured observation system is used, the expertise and pedagogical knowledge of the recorder are of little importance, and the validity of the evaluations depends mainly on the observer's skill in using the instrument.

Our recommendation is that you look for people who have had some classroom experience but have not been trained or employed as administrators or supervisors. In almost every community a potential source of observers is homemakers, mothers of small children, trained and often formerly employed as classroom teachers, who maintain a continued, active interest in education and would welcome the opportunity to work part time in the schools. Other promising prospects are people employed as substitute teachers or as teacher aides and graduate students in nearby schools of education. On the other hand, using teachers presently employed in the school (on a released-time basis) would have the advantage of broadening the teachers' involvement in the project. On the whole, we prefer outside observers because they are likely to be more disinterested and therefore more objective.

You will find that not everyone can get the knack of recording behaviors accurately and objectively, no matter how hard they try. It is therefore important to measure the observer validity of each individual recorder after training and before he is employed as a recorder. It is a good idea to train a few more observers than you need, with the understanding that only some of them will be hired. You should try also to judge which of the candidates, in addition to being competent recorders, also seem to have a clear sense of professional responsibility. One indiscreet or biased observer, one who fails to establish and maintain a relationship of mutual confidence and respect with the teachers being evaluated, could destroy the general feeling of confidence and mutual trust that is so important to the success of the program. It is not easy to develop a professional attitude in someone who does not already possess it, so the focus of selection might be on this characteristic, while that of training might be on the development of coding and recording skill.

Just as surely as abstraction is the first step in the scientific process, so (as we have seen) coding and recording behavior is an essential step in the process of performance evaluation. Coding is necessary because it is impossible to quantify a behavior record that has not been coded. Coding is, indeed, one form of abstraction. This method of abstraction involves noting, recognizing, and recording certain behaviors or categories of behavior as they occur, and disregarding all other behaviors (except to the degree that they make it easier to recognize relevant behaviors). The shorter the time between the occurrence of an event and the moment in which it is recorded, the more accurate and objective the record will be. If this interval exceeds three to five minutes, adequate objectivity is almost impossible to attain. Human memory is notoriously untrustworthy, and in that amount of time it can fade to a point at whcih the observer's general impression of the teacher will affect his recollection more than what actually happened.

Ratings are particularly subject to this kind of distortion of the particular by the general; and observers with expertise in pedagogy, experience in evaluating teachers with rating scales, or any personal or professional connection with the teacher being observed are especially susceptible to it as well. Common sense might suggest that using observers like these should increase the validity of your evaluations; the fact is that it is much more likely to have the opposite effect.

OBSERVER TRAINING

Observers must learn two important things. First, they must learn the definitions of the signs or categories in the system and the cues by which they can tell one from another. Second, they must learn to discipline themselves to disregard everything else but those cues. They must also learn such things as to make the appropriate mark in the appropriate place on the form, and the proper procedure for checking into and out of a school building, entering and leaving a classroom, and looking like part of the furniture while they are there.

Because of the nature of each different observation system and the way in which it has been developed, the procedure for training observers used with each observation system will involve materials and procedures unique to that system. If you have chosen to use a well-established system you should, of course, follow the procedures and use the materials recommended by the developers. In order for your records to be valid, it is imperative that your observers learn the operational definitions stated in those materials. Similar or identical terms are often defined differently in different systems. In the PROSE system (Medley, 1971), for instance, *cooperation* may mean pupil compliance with a teacher's request, while in Stallings' (1977) system the same term is only used to describe two pupils working together on a common task. Some knowledge of how a system evolved, how it was developed, and the rationale for developing it may help to clarify the terms, concepts, and other ideas used in the system.

Most observation systems provide detailed instruction manuals for recorders which include examples of the behaviors, and many also provide films, audiotapes, or videotapes which illustrate and clarify the definitions. Every effort should be made to train observers to code behaviors in exactly the same way as they would if they had been trained by the developers of the system, that is, to a high degree of observer validity. This is only possible if the training materials supplied include test materials—tapes or films that have been coded correctly or keyed by the developers of the system.

Once a trainee has memorized the definitions, he is ready to begin a period of practice in coding. At this phase it is particularly desirable to involve the developer of the instrument, or, if that is impossible, someone who knows the system well and is experienced in its use. In any case, conflicts or misunderstandings about definitions and procedures should be referred to some such source for resolution.

Experience in live classrooms should begin soon after the trainees are familiar with the item definitions. Live classrooms are so much more complex than videotapes that observers who work only with videotapes until they have mastered a system are likely to experience a shock when they first observe a live classroom. Live experiences can most usefully be interspersed with videotape training, even if the videotape practice carries the major load.

ESTABLISHING OBSERVER VALIDITY

Observer Validity

At this point it is appropriate to attempt to measure observer validity; that is, to ascertain how closely a record made by each observer reflects the behavior he or she is supposed to have recorded.

If a test tape or film—that is, one for which a key to correct coding is available—has been provided by the system's developer, each trainee may be asked to view it and record what he observes. The degree to which the trainee's record agrees with the key is a measure of the validity of a record made by that observer. If no test tape or film exists but an expert recorder is available, then each trainee and the expert may visit a classroom together and record the same behavior, and the two records may be compared to assess the validity of the record made by the novice. If neither of these procedures is feasible, then the trainees can visit classrooms in pairs and the degree of observer agreement can be measured.

The developers of most major systems will have established levels of observer validity which may be considered satisfactory, taking into account the complexity of the system. If not, you will have to set your own criterion. Observers who fail to meet whatever criterion is set may be allowed to study the definitions and practice a few more times and then try again. Those who cannot reach the criterion in a reasonable length of time should not be used in the program.

Percent of Observer Agreement

This statistic, which is often mistakenly interpreted as a coefficient of reliability, is most simply calculated by dividing the number of items on which two records agree by the total number of agreements possible. (For more elaborate procedures see Frick and Semmel, 1978).

Figure 7.1 illustrates a procedure that is particularly useful (Frick and Semmel, 1978; Stallings, 1977). The figure shows how a trainee coded each of 100 items on a test tape and the correct coding for each

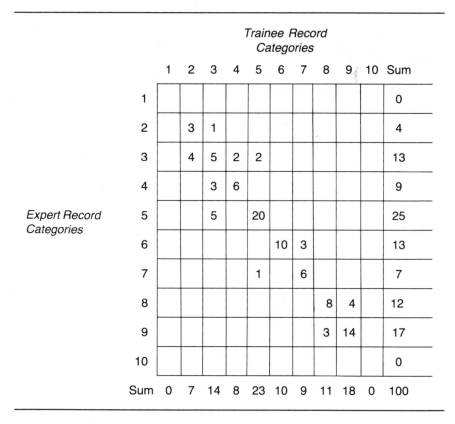

		1	2	3	4	5	6	7	8	9	10	Sum
	1											0
	2		3	1								4
	3		4	5	2	2						13
	4			3	6							9
Expert Record Categories	5			5		20						25
	6						10	3				13
	7					1		6				7
	8								8	4		12
	9								3	14		17
	10											0
	Sum	0	7	14	8	23	10	9	11	18	0	100

FIGURE 7.1   A procedure for estimating percentage of observer agreement.

item. (It should be noted that each event on the test tape was preceded by a beep on the sound track to ensure that the trainee's record was synchronized with the key.)

Notice that three events were coded 2 on both records (as indicated by the 3 in row 3, column 2). But one event (row 2, column 3) which according to the key should have been coded 2 was coded 3 by the trainee; and that four events (row 3, column 2) which should have been coded 3 were coded 2 by the trainee. We see that the trainee recorded 5 out of 13 events in category 3 correctly, or 38 percent, and that the most common error was to miscode a 3 as a 2. In this way the procedure provides information about either ambiguities in the category definitions or uncertainties of this coder, or both.

Looking at the figure as a whole, we see that the numbers on the diagonal correspond to events correctly coded by the observer, and that those off the diagonal correspond to incorrect codings. If we count them we find that 72 of the 100 tallies are on the diagonal, so we estimate that this observer's records are 72 percent accurate: the validity of the observer may be said to be .72 or 72 percent.

The simpler methods of estimating observer agreement and accuracy mentioned earlier focus on agreement in total frequencies per category rather than on agreement on individual events. They use only the marginal sums in the figure. If you compare the marginal sums of the trainee with those of the expert, you will find that the agreement between the two records is 93 percent. A substantial number of errors seem to have canceled each other out. If you had used the simpler method you would have missed the information about the difficulties the trainee was having with category 3 or in distinguishing between categories 5 and 3.

When your corps of observers is complete, you should provide some opportunity for them to practice observing in classes similar to those they will visit as part of the evaluation program. They should make these visits in pairs so that they can review and compare their records, and the composition of the pairs should be changed frequently. One or two sessions in which the entire group gets together and discusses questions or disagreements will also be helpful. Each observer's validity should be rechecked from time to time, particularly whenever a new series of observations are to be made after a period of idleness, and refresher training provided as needed.

Most developers of instruments have had enough experience in training observers to be able to provide information about the most satisfactory kind of training as well as the time required to learn the instrument. It might be helpful to know that this particular type of training is usually done in a number of relatively short time periods spread over a number of days. For example, the *Teacher Practices Observation Record* (TPOR) manual recommends five two-hour sessions extended over at least a five-day period (Brown, 1970). A more sophisticated observation system such as STARS, the *Spaulding Teacher Activity Recording Schedule* (Spaulding, 1970), requires much more extensive training, usually over a period of several weeks, even months. Observer training should be organized so that all trainees have an opportunity to be together to discuss and interact as they seek to reach agreement among themselves, and with the expert observer who is leading the training.

To summarize, then, observers should attempt to understand the developer's rationale and objectives for the instrument, what the categories, signs, or classifications that are being used mean, and if possible, why the system is organized as it is. Observers should then memorize the definitions as presented without attempting to interpret or to apply other definitions. Finally, the observers should practice recording until they feel comfortable with every item on the instrument and are able to locate each item on the instrument instantly.

To repeat an earlier recommendation, to the degree that it is feasible all participants in the study, though they will not collect any data and are being trained for other reasons, should participate in all phases of the observer training.

COLLECTING THE DATA

The Sample

One of the first problems you will face when you begin to plan a series of observations to be used for evaluative purposes is deciding what kind of a sample of observations of each teacher you will need. You will need to answer questions like the following: How many observations per teacher should you schedule? When should you schedule them? How long should each visit last? It seems likely that, because of the instability of human behavior in general, and of teaching behavior in particular, one visit will not usually be enough; scores based on records of single visits to each teacher will probably not be reliable enough to be useful. But how many visits will you need? Until you have collected some reliability data with your own observers, your own instrument, and your own teachers you will not be able to answer this question definitively, but you will have to make some tentative answer before you can start evaluating.

The answer will depend to some extent on which observation instrument you are using, which suggests that the technical manual or users' manual for the system you are using (if one exists) may be of some help. It will probably contain a flexible set of guidelines as to the number and length of visits that are necessary for objective, stable, reliable and valid data collection according to the authors' experience. Since this experience will usually have been gained in research studies rather than in an evaluation program, the recommendations should be regarded as tentative, but they should help.

If you are using an instrument you have constructed yourself, there will of course be no such help available. In that case you should try to benefit from what you can find out about other instruments similar to yours. For instance, the developers of the CCS, a sign system, recommend that two or more observers visit each classroom at different times, and make a series of three, five-minute observations per visit (Soar and Soar, 1982). The authors of another sign system, COKER, suggest that each observer record behaviors on the first of the two parts of the system (called the matrix) for five minutes, and then pause and record as many of the signs listed in the second part as were observed during the same five minutes. This completes one observation; the authors report that highly reliable scores can be obtained with six visits and two observations per visit. Other users of COKER report satisfactory results from four visits with four observations per visit.

There is a recommendation we can make which does not depend on what instrument you choose to use. Whatever number of visits you decide to make to each teacher, your best strategy is to train and use at least that many observers, so that each visit to any single teacher can be made by a different observer. We also recommend that, if at all possible, you schedule one trial visit to each classroom before the first visit for evaluative purposes. This will give both the teacher and the class an opportunity to get accustomed to being observed, and at the same time will give your observers a chance to get used to observing.

Observer Effects

Observer effects on the behavior of teachers and pupils have been the subject of much speculation and concern among researchers and their critics; but this concern has produced very little empirical research, probably because it is so difficult to get reliable observations of what happens in a classroom when no one is there to observe!

Whether an observer is present or not seems to have relatively little effect on the behaviors of pupils, once they get over the initial curiosity aroused when the observer first appears. We have seen a class of pupils misbehave energetically while their teacher is temporarily absent, even posting a monitor at the door to warn the class of her return, with complete disregard for the observer sitting in the corner making marks on his clipboard all the while.

Knowing that they are being evaluated makes some teachers so nervous that they do not perform well enough to do themselves justice. This phenomenon is not peculiar to teaching. Test anxiety can and does strike some of those taking almost any kind of test. The problem is well known, and has no simple solution. However, this is not the problem that causes most of the concern about observer effects on teacher performance. What concerns people most is the possibility that the teacher being observed may alter her behavior and get a better evaluation than she deserves.

We know of only one empirical study of the difference between the behavior of teachers when they know they are being observed and their behavior when they do not know they are being observed (Samph, 1976). When teachers knew that what they said was being recorded, observers using Flanders' system (Flanders, 1970) recorded more positive affect and more indirect teaching than they recorded when the teachers did not know that what they said was being recorded. Although statistically significant, the differences were quite small in magnitude. But these teachers knew that even when they were being observed they were not being evaluated, so the pressure on them to do their best was probably much weaker than it would otherwise have been.

This problem should not concern you too much, even though your observations will be made for the purpose of assessing teacher competence. Competence has to do with teacher ability, with the best that the teacher is *able* to do, not with what she does every day. The observation situation is a test situation like any other. In any other test situation the person taking the test would be expected and encouraged to do her best. Indeed, it is generally understood that a test can yield valid measurements only when the person being tested is motivated to do his or her very best. The custom many raters follow of asking the teacher to "go right on with whatever you are doing, and try to act as if I were not here" asks the teacher to give up her basic right to do her best whenever her ability to do anything is being assessed.

RELIABILITY AND OBSERVER AGREEMENT

A key point which does not seem to be widely realized is the distinction between the reliability of a score based on one or more observational records and the amount of agreement between records of the same behavior made by different observers. Not only are the coefficient of reliability of a score and the percent of observer agreement on an instrument calculated in different ways; they also pertain to quite different properties of observational data.

The coefficient of reliability estimates a property of a *score* derived from one or more observational records. It is an index of how well the score discriminates between teachers, that is, detects stable differences between them. The coefficient of reliability of a score is an index of the degree to which scores based on two different sets of records of behavior of a group of teachers rank the teachers in the same order. A perfectly reliable score would have a coefficient of reliability equal to 1.00, and any two sets of scores would rank the teachers in the same order, no matter when the records were made or by whom. Reliability is, of course, a matter of degree, and no perfectly reliable scoring key exists; but scores with coefficients of reliability as high as .80 or so are not unusual.

The percent of observer agreement normally has no direct relationship to any particular score derived from an observational record; it has to do with the items or categories observers use in recording behavior and the extent to which their frequencies agree on records of the same behavior made by different observers. It is a direct function of what we have called *observer validity*, which means the degree to which the frequencies in an observer's record agree with the actual frequencies of occurrence of the items or categories of behavior recorded, and is used as a measure of observer validity.

How high the percent of observer agreement is depends on the clarity of the definitions of the items or categories the observers must use, how observable the cues the observer must use in coding are, and how well the observers have been trained. The reliability of a score also depends on these things to a degree, but it depends much more on the internal consistency of the scoring key, the stability of whatever aspect of behavior the score measures, and the range of variation among the teachers to be evaluated.

Some writers regard the average percent of observer agreement on an instrument as an index or measure of the reliability of the *instrument*, but this does not make sense since there is no such thing. We sometimes speak of the reliability of a paper-and-pencil test when what we are really talking about is the reliability of a *score* on the test. This careless way of speaking causes very little confusion because the test has only one score. But an observation schedule usually yields several scores on as many different dimensions, some of which may be reliable and some not. The confusion created by speaking of instrument reliability (which does not exist) is compounded when it is the percent of agreement that is referred to. This is particularly unfortunate when (as is usually the case) the observer agreement on a system is high but the reliabilities of scores obtained from it are low.

The following not-too-serious example will illustrate the difference between the two measures. Suppose that one of the items on an instrument is *teacher levitates*. If two observers were to visit a number of classrooms together, they would probably agree 100 percent on the frequency of occurrence of this event in each classroom because it was zero in each. Suppose also that a key made up entirely of such items was scored on the instrument. Despite the perfect observer agreement the reliability of scores on the key would be zero, since they failed to discriminate among the teachers because there was no variability to detect. To report that this instrument was highly reliable would give a wrong impression of its usefulness for evaluating teachers.

Another misunderstanding arises in the case of behaviorally anchored rating scales like the TPAI (Capie et al., 1979). A behaviorally anchored rating scale lists behaviors typical of teachers rated at different levels, and instructs the rater to rate a teacher at whatever level her behavior resembles most closely. Does the fact that two observers rate a teacher at the same level on the same item mean that both of them saw the same behavior occur? In other words, is it evidence that the behavior record is accurate?

As we noted in Chapter 3, factor analyses of records made on behaviorally anchored rating scales like the TPAI strongly indicate that such ratings are determined more by the observer's general impression of how competent the teacher is than by which of the "anchoring behaviors" actually occurred during the observation (cf. Dickson and Wiersma, 1980; Dickson et al. 1982). Raters who form the same overall impression of a teacher but observe different behaviors are at least as likely to assign the same rating to a teacher as raters who form different overall impressions but observe the same behaviors.

ESTABLISHING THE RELIABILITY OF A BEHAVIORAL MEASURE

It may be worth emphasizing once more how important it is to know how reliable the scores are that you obtain with your observers, your instrument, and your teachers. Most of us know that the reliability of a measure depends on the internal consistency of the scoring key used to obtain it, and on the stability of the competency or other dimension of performance being measured, as well as on the validities of your observers. We tend to forget that it also depends on what your teachers are like—on how much of that competency the average teacher possesses and especially on the range of the competency in the group. It is not difficult to see that no measure can be reliable, can discriminate between teachers if there are no differences between them to detect.

It is therefore important, as soon as you have enough data to do so, that you estimate the reliability of the data you are collecting. Reliability information is important, first of all, for planning the kind of a sample of teacher behavior you will need. And as we shall see in the next chapter, it also provides information necessary to plan efforts to improve the quality of the measures you obtain by revising and refining the scoring procedures you use.

There are four statistics, any one of which might be and has been called a reliability coefficient, with some claim to legitimacy. They are: the *coefficient of observer agreement*, the *coefficient of stability*, the *coefficient of internal consistency*, and the *Reliability Coefficient* (which we will capitalize to distinguish it from the other three coefficients).

Each of these four coefficients is defined as the correlation between different sets of scores of the same group of teachers obtained on the same scoring key. The four coefficients differ in how the different sets of scores of the same teachers are obtained in each instance.

Shanker, Albert. Personal communication, June 9, 1983.

Smith, B. O. *A Design for a School of Pedagogy*. Washington, DC: United States Department of Education, 1980, publ. no. E-80-42000.

Soar, Robert S., and Ruth M. Soar. *Climate and Control System*. Gainesville, FL: College of Education, University of Florida, 1982.

Spaulding, Robert L. *Spaulding Teacher Activity Rating Schedule (STARS)*. San Jose, CA: San Jose State University, 1970.

Stallings, J. A. *Learning to Look: A Handbook on Classroom Observation and Teaching Models*. Belmont, CA: Wadsworth, 1977.

The Coefficient of Observer Agreement. This statistic (like all those discussed in this section) pertains to a score or measure based on an observational record, and should not be confused with the percent of observer agreement discussed earlier, which pertains to the individual behavior items or categories recorded. A coefficient of observer agreement is estimated by correlating scores based on records made by different observers observing the same behaviors. The coefficient of observer agreement is attenuated only by errors made by observers in recording behaviors.

The Coefficient of Stability. This statistic is estimated by correlating scores based on records made by the same observer in the same classrooms on different occasions. The occasions should, of course, be ones when the tasks that the teacher is supposed to perform are equivalent, and should be chosen to be typical of such occasions. The stability coefficient may be thought of as analogous to the "test-retest reliability" of a test; it is attenuated only by errors due to variations in the behavior of the same teacher from one occasion to another, that is, to instability of teacher performance.

The Coefficient of Internal Consistency. Estimates of this coefficent are based on the intercorrelations between scores on different items on the same scoring key on the same record; that is, the records used to estimate this statistic are records made by the same observer during the same period of observation on different items. It corresponds to coefficients of internal consistency of tests estimated from "split-halves" or one of the Kuder-Richardson formulas. This coefficient is attenuated only by variations in the degree to which different items on a scoring key measure the same dimension of performance.

Although internal consistency coefficients are used more often than any others as evidence of the reliabilities of paper-and-pencil tests, their usefulness with observational measures is generally limited to the kinds of internal analyses of scoring keys that will be discussed in Chapter 8. We shall therefore disregard them in the remainder of the present discussion.

The Reliability Coefficient. What we will call the Reliability Coefficient is estimated by correlating scores based on records made by different observers on different occasions in the same classrooms, occasions in which the teachers are working at equivalent tasks. It will normally be smaller than either the coefficient of observer agreement or the coefficient of stability of a measure because it is attenuated both by observer errors and by instability of performance.

Whenever you evaluate teacher competence by observing teacher performance the reliability of your assessments will be attenuated or reduced by errors of both types. If you attempt to estimate how reliable one of your measures is by using either a coefficient of observer agreement or a coefficient of stability, you will overestimate the reliability of a score and underestimate the amount of error it contains. It is important, therefore, to use the Reliability Coefficient rather than either of these substitutes.

One final point. Pearson's product-moment coefficient of correlation is still widely used to estimate the reliabilities of paper-and-pencil tests, although it was long ago shown that this is not the best formula to use (Jackson, 1939; Jackson and Ferguson, 1941). Pearson's formula yields an estimate that is satisfactory for most purposes, so long as there are only two sets of scores to be correlated. But when (as often happens when you are dealing with observational scores) you have three or more scores per teacher to correlate, or when two or more different kinds of errors are involved, it does not yield a satisfactory estimate. Furthermore, the product-moment correlation is insensitive to observer differences in average scores. To illustrate, assume that two observers put a group of teachers in the same rank order with respect to the amount of negative affect they express, but assume that one regularly sees more affect (gives higher scores) than the other. Product-moment correlation takes account of the agreement in order, but ignores the difference in average score between observers. If different teachers are visited by different observers, as is usually the case, then the statistical procedure used should produce lower reliability estimates to the degree that such observer differences are present.

The appropriate statistic to use is known as the *intraclass correlation coefficient*. It is most conveniently estimated from an analysis of variance appropriate to the design used in the data collection (Bartko, 1976; Rowley, 1976). For a brief discussion of the topic see Medley and Mitzel (1963); for a more thorough treatment of "generalizability theory" (as it is called today) see Brennan (1983). A general-purpose design for estimating the reliability of scores based on classroom observation records is presented in Appendix B.

SUMMARY

In this chapter we have attempted to identify the procedures which will enable you to obtain an objective record of teachers' performance. These procedures include observer recruitment, selection and training, how to establish observer validity and collect the data.

Because the difference between reliability and observer agreement is

not well understood, we have discussed the subject rat. as well as how to establish the reliability of a behavior.

Finally, the four statistics usually identified with re been enumerated, defined, and compared. Appendix B general-purpose design and statistical procedures for est. reliability of scores based on classroom observation records

BIBLIOGRAPHY

Amidon, E. J., and J. B. Hough, eds. *Interaction Analysis: Theory Resea. Application*. Reading, MA: Addison-Wesley, 1967.

Bartko, J. J. "On Various Intraclass Correlation Reliability Coefficients." *Ps logical Bulletin*, 1976, 83, 762–765.

Brennan, R. L. *Elements of Generalizability Theory*. Iowa City, IA: Ameri College Testing Program, 1983.

Brown, B. B. "Experimentalism in Teaching Practice." *Journal of Research a. Development in Education*, 1970, 4, 14–22.

Capie, W. et al. *Teacher Performance Assessment Instruments*. Athens, GA: Uni versity of Georgia, School of Education, 1979, ED183518.

Dickson, G. E., S. G. Jurs, J. Wenig, and W. Wiersma. "The Analysis and Interpretation of Student Teacher Observation Data Used for Measuring Teacher Competencies." Paper read at American Educational Research Association meeting, New York, March, 1982.

Dickson, G. E., and W. Wiersma. *Research and Evaluation in Teacher Education: A Concern for Competent, Effective Teachers*. Toledo, OH: The University of Toledo, May, 1980.

Flanders, N. A. *Analyzing Teaching Behavior*. Reading, MA: Addison-Wesley, 1970.

Frick, T., and M. I. Semmel. "Observer Agreement and Reliabilities of Class-room Observational Measures." *Review of Educational Research*, 1978, 48, 157–187.

Jackson, R. W. B. "Reliability of Mental Tests." *British Journal of Psychology*, 1939, 29, 267–287.

Jackson, R. W. B., and G. A. Ferguson. *Studies on the Reliability of Tests*. Toronto: Department of Educational Research, University of Toronto, 1941.

Medley, Donald M. "The Language of Teacher Behavior: Communicating the Results of Structured Observations to Teachers." *Journal of Teacher Education*, 1971, 22, 157–165.

Medley, Donald M., and Harold E. Mitzel. "Measuring Classroom Behavior by Systematic Observation." In N. L. Gage, ed., *Handbook of Research on Teaching*. Chicago, IL: Rand McNally, 1963.

Rowley, G. L. "Reliability of Observational Measures." *American Educational Research Journal*, 1976, 13, 51–59.

Samph, T. "Observer Effects on Teacher Behavior." *Journal of Educational Psychology*, 1976, 68, 736–741.

The Coefficient of Observer Agreement. This statistic (like all those discussed in this section) pertains to a score or measure based on an observational record, and should not be confused with the percent of observer agreement discussed earlier, which pertains to the individual behavior items or categories recorded. A coefficient of observer agreement is estimated by correlating scores based on records made by different observers observing the same behaviors. The coefficient of observer agreement is attenuated only by errors made by observers in recording behaviors.

The Coefficient of Stability. This statistic is estimated by correlating scores based on records made by the same observer in the same classrooms on different occasions. The occasions should, of course, be ones when the tasks that the teacher is supposed to perform are equivalent, and should be chosen to be typical of such occasions. The stability coefficient may be thought of as analogous to the "test-retest reliability" of a test; it is attenuated only by errors due to variations in the behavior of the same teacher from one occasion to another, that is, to instability of teacher performance.

The Coefficient of Internal Consistency. Estimates of this coefficent are based on the intercorrelations between scores on different items on the same scoring key on the same record; that is, the records used to estimate this statistic are records made by the same observer during the same period of observation on different items. It corresponds to coefficients of internal consistency of tests estimated from "split-halves" or one of the Kuder-Richardson formulas. This coefficient is attenuated only by variations in the degree to which different items on a scoring key measure the same dimension of performance.

Although internal consistency coefficients are used more often than any others as evidence of the reliabilities of paper-and-pencil tests, their usefulness with observational measures is generally limited to the kinds of internal analyses of scoring keys that will be discussed in Chapter 8. We shall therefore disregard them in the remainder of the present discussion.

The Reliability Coefficient. What we will call the Reliability Coefficient is estimated by correlating scores based on records made by different observers on different occasions in the same classrooms, occasions in which the teachers are working at equivalent tasks. It will normally be smaller than either the coefficient of observer agreement or the coefficient of stability of a measure because it is attenuated both by observer errors and by instability of performance.

Whenever you evaluate teacher competence by observing teacher performance the reliability of your assessments will be attenuated or reduced by errors of both types. If you attempt to estimate how reliable one of your measures is by using either a coefficient of observer agreement or a coefficient of stability, you will overestimate the reliability of a score and underestimate the amount of error it contains. It is important, therefore, to use the Reliability Coefficient rather than either of these substitutes.

One final point. Pearson's product-moment coefficient of correlation is still widely used to estimate the reliabilities of paper-and-pencil tests, although it was long ago shown that this is not the best formula to use (Jackson, 1939; Jackson and Ferguson, 1941). Pearson's formula yields an estimate that is satisfactory for most purposes, so long as there are only two sets of scores to be correlated. But when (as often happens when you are dealing with observational scores) you have three or more scores per teacher to correlate, or when two or more different kinds of errors are involved, it does not yield a satisfactory estimate. Furthermore, the product-moment correlation is insensitive to observer differences in average scores. To illustrate, assume that two observers put a group of teachers in the same rank order with respect to the amount of negative affect they express, but assume that one regularly sees more affect (gives higher scores) than the other. Product-moment correlation takes account of the agreement in order, but ignores the difference in average score between observers. If different teachers are visited by different observers, as is usually the case, then the statistical procedure used should produce lower reliability estimates to the degree that such observer differences are present.

The appropriate statistic to use is known as the *intraclass correlation coefficient*. It is most conveniently estimated from an analysis of variance appropriate to the design used in the data collection (Bartko, 1976; Rowley, 1976). For a brief discussion of the topic see Medley and Mitzel (1963); for a more thorough treatment of "generalizability theory" (as it is called today) see Brennan (1983). A general-purpose design for estimating the reliability of scores based on classroom observation records is presented in Appendix B.

SUMMARY

In this chapter we have attempted to identify the procedures which will enable you to obtain an objective record of teachers' performance. These procedures include observer recruitment, selection and training, how to establish observer validity and collect the data.

Because the difference between reliability and observer agreement is not well understood, we have discussed the subject rather thoroughly, as well as how to establish the reliability of a behavioral measure.

Finally, the four statistics usually identified with reliability have been enumerated, defined, and compared. Appendix B provides a general-purpose design and statistical procedures for estimating the reliability of scores based on classroom observation records.

BIBLIOGRAPHY

Amidon, E. J., and J. B. Hough, eds. *Interaction Analysis: Theory Research and Application.* Reading, MA: Addison-Wesley, 1967.

Bartko, J. J. "On Various Intraclass Correlation Reliability Coefficients." *Psychological Bulletin,* 1976, *83,* 762–765.

Brennan, R. L. *Elements of Generalizability Theory.* Iowa City, IA: American College Testing Program, 1983.

Brown, B. B. "Experimentalism in Teaching Practice." *Journal of Research and Development in Education,* 1970, *4,* 14–22.

Capie, W. et al. *Teacher Performance Assessment Instruments.* Athens, GA: University of Georgia, School of Education, 1979, ED183518.

Dickson, G. E., S. G. Jurs, J. Wenig, and W. Wiersma. "The Analysis and Interpretation of Student Teacher Observation Data Used for Measuring Teacher Competencies." Paper read at American Educational Research Association meeting, New York, March, 1982.

Dickson, G. E., and W. Wiersma. *Research and Evaluation in Teacher Education: A Concern for Competent, Effective Teachers.* Toledo, OH: The University of Toledo, May, 1980.

Flanders, N. A. *Analyzing Teaching Behavior.* Reading, MA: Addison-Wesley, 1970.

Frick, T., and M. I. Semmel. "Observer Agreement and Reliabilities of Classroom Observational Measures." *Review of Educational Research,* 1978, *48,* 157–187.

Jackson, R. W. B. "Reliability of Mental Tests." *British Journal of Psychology,* 1939, *29,* 267–287.

Jackson, R. W. B., and G. A. Ferguson. *Studies on the Reliability of Tests.* Toronto: Department of Educational Research, University of Toronto, 1941.

Medley, Donald M. "The Language of Teacher Behavior: Communicating the Results of Structured Observations to Teachers." *Journal of Teacher Education,* 1971, *22,* 157–165.

Medley, Donald M., and Harold E. Mitzel. "Measuring Classroom Behavior by Systematic Observation." In N. L. Gage, ed., *Handbook of Research on Teaching.* Chicago, IL: Rand McNally, 1963.

Rowley, G. L. "Reliability of Observational Measures." *American Educational Research Journal,* 1976, *13,* 51–59.

Samph, T. "Observer Effects on Teacher Behavior." *Journal of Educational Psychology,* 1976, *68,* 736–741.

Shanker, Albert. Personal communication, June 9, 1983.

Smith, B. O. *A Design for a School of Pedagogy*. Washington, DC: United States Department of Education, 1980, publ. no. E-80-42000.

Soar, Robert S., and Ruth M. Soar. *Climate and Control System*. Gainesville, FL: College of Education, University of Florida, 1982.

Spaulding, Robert L. *Spaulding Teacher Activity Rating Schedule (STARS)*. San Jose, CA: San Jose State University, 1970.

Stallings, J. A. *Learning to Look: A Handbook on Classroom Observation and Teaching Models*. Belmont, CA: Wadsworth, 1977.